View of *Sante Marie Among the Iroquois* on Onondaga Lake

Sainte Marie
among
the
Iroquois

A Living History Museum
of the French and the Iroquois
at Onondaga
in the 17th Century.

Elizabeth Metz

Printed by
Midgley Printing Inc.
200 Oxford Street
Syracuse, New York 13202

Distributed by
Friends of Historic Onondaga Lake
PO Box 146 Liverpool, NY 13088

Contents

Illustrations

Scenes at Living History Site

Jesuit at the Chapel

Chickens at the Wattle Fence

A French Soldier

ACKNOWLEDGEMENTS

In the preparation of this book I am indebted to Robert Geraci, Director, and Valerie Bell, Curator, at *Sainte Marie* for their advice, suggestions and support.; to Rev. Raymond Bucko, S. J. LeMoyne college for his careful reading of the manuscript and many suggestions; to the staff of the computer lab at Liverpool Library, LeMoyne College Library and Syracuse University Library for their aid; to my husband for his patience and support.. However, errors and omissions are my responsibility. It should be noted that Dennis J. Connors was director of the Office of Museums and Historic Sites at the Onondaga County Parks and Recreation Department when replacing the "French Fort" was being considered. He is responsible for the development of *Sainte Marie Among the Iroquois*. It was his perseverance in achieving his vision of the living history museum that makes this 17th century site live today.

Part I: Guide to Sainte Marie Among the Iroquois

Land of the Onondagas

Visitors to *Sainte Marie* enter a two-story atrium that rises forty feet. It is a life-sized diorama of the forests, water and wildlife in the Onondaga Lake region when the French arrived in the 17th century.

Special cases hold projectile points, pottery, and tools made of stone, bone and antlers that were found on archeological sites near Sainte Marie. They show some of the ways natural materials were used before the Europeans arrived.

The turtle sculpture, by Iroquois Tom Huff, depicts the clan animals and the Great Tree of Peace. A bronze head of the great chief To-do-da-ho and a bronze sculpture of the Creator's Game, lacrosse, also greet the visitor.

Elm Bark Canoe

Suspended above the circular stairway leading to the second level, is an elm-bark canoe with a life-size figure representing an Onondaga about to spear an eel. A bald eagle soars above wood ducks and passenger pigeons (now extinct). A life-size black bear, a timber wolf, and a rattlesnake (supplied by the Department of Environmental Conservation from roadkills) are part of the background. The sounds of the forest are all around with the call of the birds, the animals and the insects.

Iroquois Art

Paintings by Iroquois artists line the balcony. One, depicting Onondaga Lake, recalls for the Iroquois that long before the Europeans arrived, the Peacemaker came to unite the Mohawk, the Oneida, the Onondaga, the Cayuga, and the Seneca as the Hau-de-no-sau-nee, or the People of the Longhouse, as they called themselves. Others refer to them as the Iroquois Confederacy. Hidden within the painting are the clan animals (bear, wolf, turtle, eel, deer, beaver, snipe, and the hawk), a longhouse and the peacemaker's canoe.

1

The Great Tree of Peace

On the shore of Onondaga Lake the Peacemaker uprooted a great pine tree and buried the weapons of war beneath its roots and then replanted the tree. He burned sacred tobacco as part of the ritual. At the re-opening of *Sainte Marie Among the Iroquois* on August 10, 1991, representatives of the Iroquois Confederacy joined with community leaders to plant a pine tree at the entrance to the museum. Onondaga Chief Irving Powless stated that "This is for peace, not only on the shores of Onondaga Lake, but throughout the world."

Iroquois Creation Story

A second painting interprets the Iroquois Creation Story with the turtle on whose back North America was placed, the Three Sisters, corn, beans and squash, given by the Creator and Grandmother Moon watching over all.

Another painting explains the traditional division of time during the year. The cycle, controlled by the moon, has a special ceremony of celebration for each period. It begins with the flow of maple sap in the spring, the seasons to plant, the ripening of the strawberry, the harvests of different crops and finally the rekindling of the winter fires, a time to honor mother Earth and renew ancient beliefs. And then another new year's arrival is celebrated.

A fourth painting graphically depicts the Great Thanksgiving Address still given today by the Iroquois at important ceremonies to open public gatherings. In the painting a man and woman stand on the red path that symbolizes the "Lifeline of Mother Earth." The circles contain images of the following:

The Land on which we walk...
Grasses that provide medicine...
Sweet strawberries that renew people...
Trees that provide fuel and protection...
Water to refresh the land, animals and people...
Animals for food and clothing...
Birds for song and beauty...
The Three Sisters, corn, beans, and squash to
  sustain the people

2

The Wind that brings the seasons...
Elder Brother the Sun that lights and warms the day
Grandmother Moon that lights the night...
The Stars that guide in the night...
The four Sacred Messengers from the Creator..
The Peace of the Iroquois Confederacy symbolized
    by the five wampum strings...
Above the couple is the sky dome and the ever
    watchful eagle.

The Europeans Arrive

At the entrance to the second floor exhibits, a section of a sailing ship's deck has been recreated. Discover how and why the Europeans came to this land in small, wooden sailing ships. Seated in a bunk, listen to a tape of letters from a ship's captain and from a Jesuit priest as they describe their voyages. Nearby are barrels with trade goods and food for the voyage. Open a door to learn more about the ships that sailed 300 years ago. Examine the maps which show the routes of people coming from all over Europe. A timeline gives the history.

Two wall murals depict 17th century daily life, one in a French village, and the other in an Iroquois village. Behind small doors discover the differences and similarities in the two cultures.

Attend a Treaty

The next exhibit shows two life-sized figures discussing the treaty that created *Sainte Marie*. On a tape, hear Chief Garakontie's invitation to the French and Governor Lauzon's reply. A timeline from 1649 to 1657 lists important events in world news at the time.

Watch a Video of Global News Network

Next, let a newscast take you back in time as you listen to an interview on the imaginary "Global News Network." After noting the current events in England about Oliver Cromwell, and the war between France and Spain, the reporter goes "live" to the St. Lawrence River to cover the departure of the men about to make the long trip from Montreal to *Sainte Marie*.

Enter the Mission

Leaving the Visitor Center go along a path that winds through a treed area to represent the original forest and vegetable garden.

Within the palisaded compound of the mission, chickens roam free. Pigs lie behind a wattle fence. The animals are breeds that date from 17th Century Europe. Visit the kitchen/dining hall. The cook will answer questions about life at the mission.

Near the chapel a black-robed Jesuit will tell you why they came to the Onondagas.

The carpenter may be hewing beams, making a chair or table, or explaining how to use his tools.

Nearby the blacksmith can often be found at the forge molding nails or repairing some of the iron tools they carried all the way from France. Visit the barracks that house the French.

The methods used by these craftsmen are authentic to this period of French-Canadian building. They were determined by a careful synthesis of data from similar sites and compared to the brief information available on the original Onondaga mission.

Return to the Visitor Center

As you leave the mission, follow the path through the garden. You will find the corn, beans, and squash growing as the Onondagas taught the French. A fish is planted with the seed for fertilizer. The corn stalks hold the vines for the beans and squash. You may find a log being made into a canoe by an Onondaga. He will be hollowing it with fire. When you enter the Visitor Center, descend to the first floor.

At the exit, a gift shop offers many interesting items.

Building the Replicas of Sainte Marie

That first replica, *Sainte Marie de Gannentaha,* was constructed in 1933 as part of a Works Progress Administration Program to develop the 300-acre Onondaga Lake Parkway on former salt reservation land between Syracuse and Liverpool. One hundred fifty unemployed carpenters, architects, and other craftsmen were paid twenty-five cents per hour to clear and grade the land and build the mission under the supervision of Architect Howell Richardson.

The present *Sainte Marie Among the Iroquois* was opened on April 10, 1991, as a living history museum. As the only historic French site of that period in the United States, it replaces what was popularly called the "French Fort."

The Old "French Fort"

The original replica was 110 feet long and 85 feet wide. Buildings served as part of the stockade. They included a barracks along the length of one side between two bastions, a house for the Jesuit fathers and one for Mons. Dupuis, who

6

commanded the soldiers, and a storehouse, a forge shop, a kitchen and bake shop. A palisade connected the intervening space between the walls of the buildings. American Indian artifacts and other furnishings were originally displayed in the interiors. However, many disappeared due to fire, thieves and vandals.

Over the years various civic groups took an interest in the "French Fort," as it was known. In 1965, the members of six local Kiwanis clubs refurbished all the rooms on the inside. They installed an electric line to the fort and arranged for plaques to describe the use of each room. 50,000 illustrated brochures were printed for students and visitors.

For forty years this first replica of *Sainte Marie* had only a special watchman as staff, William Gallipeau. Except for the three years he served in World War II, he offered background information to visitors.

In 1974, as part of its plan for the Bicentennial Celebration, the Onondaga County Parks Department decided to maintain the "French Fort" as a working museum with staff members in period costume performing the crafts of 17th Century France. However, the buildings had severely deteriorated. In addition, recent historical and archeological work on 17th Century French Canadian sites revealed that the old log cabin style was not historically accurate in design. Thus, plans were made to renovate it

Planning a New *Sainte Marie*

Many have speculated that the original *Sainte Marie* was located on old Liverpool Road at the present site of Le Moyne Manor Restaurant, formerly the house of Ward Wellington Ward, noted local architect. At the time of its construction in 1916, many colonial artifacts were reportedly found during the excavation. They were on display in his home for many years, but have unfortunately disappeared. Other items found on the site at an earlier time included glass trade beads, a stone effigy, enamelled beads, and a silver coin depicting Louis XIII who reigned 1610-1643. (Connors, 1980, 49-50).

The actual site examined as the location of the original *Sainte Marie* is a portion of lot 106 in the Town of Salina,

Onondaga County, New York. It was identified in a 1797 survey of the Onondaga Lake area conducted by James Geddes. The original map shows all of Onondaga Lake, and outlines, in rather crude detail, a main structure approximately 100' square, according to the scale present. . . . The whole structure is clearly labeled the "Old Stockade." Nearby, so close as to touch the extension, a substantial spring of distinctive shape, is indicated, flowing into the Lake (Connors, 18). It can still be seen and is known as the Jesuit Well.

The 100' square stockade with defensive units or "parapets" at each corner is an example of a basic fortification design that would have been familiar to both the military commander, Major Zacharie Dupuis, and his religious counterpart, Rev. Francois le Mercier. A square with four corner towers had been used in Europe for centuries (Connors, 21).

The overall size and configuration of the ruins are not inconsistent with the size and arrangement of the north and south courts as excavated at *Ste. Marie Among the Hurons.* Both the Huron site and the Onondaga Lake stockade are essentially square compounds, fortified with square corner bastions and adjoined by isosceles-shaped sub-compounds.

Archeological excavations

Archeological excavations at the site of the "Old Stockade" on the 1797 survey map were conducted in 1974 and 1979 by the William M. Beauchamp Chapter of the New York State Archaeological Association.

Most of the artifacts recovered related to the 19th and 20th centuries. However, those of the 17th century included three glass trade beads and a European ball clay pipe bowl that was probably Dutch of the early 1600's. Other items included a gun hammer, a gunflint, and two pieces of lead shot. The gun hammer is from a flintlock musket distinctively of the type used in the 1640-1660 period. It was so rusty that the shape of the back of it could not be clearly made out. Through the kindness of NYSAA Beauchamp Chapter member and, dentist by profession, Dr. A Gregory Schrweide, the item was X-rayed. Beneath the rust, the outline was discerned and revealed a

8

straight back and the notch for the "dog" of a doglock musket, both distinctively 1640-1660 in character.

The gunflint is made of a white mottled black flint. Macroscopically, the flint is unidentifiable as to source and a thin section was not made of it. It has a modified spall form ("D" shaped, 24mm wide at front edge, 19mm long and about 44mm thick). The small size of the flint indicated that it is likely from a light fusil or pistol, which the form suggests 17th century vintage (Connors, 41).

The 1974 and 1979 excavations revealed evidence of a section of one wall of a preserved fortification, or the wall of a building. This evidence consisted of a string of 3 to 5 inch diameter post molds running (however interruptedly), a distance of c. 20 feet. The northernmost end of this line revealed a large number of burned rocks with small particles of charcoal scattered in and amongst them. This rock-strewn area suggests chimney or, even more likely, a burned bastion. Opposite this area, on the east wall of the excavation can be seen a lens of burned soil suggesting where a shallow trench in which a wall of logs might have been set as part of the matrix to the wall of the fort.

Another kind of structure of particular interest was a flat-bottomed pit which contained gray, ashy clay and 17th century artifacts within the first two inches from its surface.

Of considerable importance is the fact that the post molds and the features bearing 17th or 18th century materials lay in a black ashy layer one to two inches thick . . . The post molds and the other features may therefore be safely assigned a date of 18th century or earlier (Connors, 51).

The site shown on the Geddes map of 1797, presently located at and adjacent to present Le Moyne Manor Restaurant is, on the basis of documentation, the most likely candidate for the site of *Ste. Marie de Gannentaha* Mission.

Appearance of Mission

No definitive details on the appearance of *Ste. Marie* were found in a literature search. However, the Province of Ontario conducted extensive archaeological investigation of the site of the *Ste. Marie Among the Hurons* occupied from 1639 to 1649. Their reconstruction of the mission depicts a complex of several specialized buildings including residence, barn, animal yards, a chapel, work shops and elements of basic military fortification, located on high ground with nearby fields. Charles Boivin, under life contract to the Jesuits, was the master builder responsible for the construction of *Ste. Marie among the Hurons* and was at *Ste. Marie de Gannentaha.* However, without clear evidence, the particular construction technique employed at *Ste Marie* cannot be determined (Connors,14).

The 1980 report summarized the two digs plus all existing documentary sources and concluded that something was there. All evidence pointed to *Sainte Marie.*

The Onondaga County Parks Department in late 1982, obtained a federal grant of $20,000 to develop a plan for a new *Sainte Marie.* A private group, Friends of Historic Onondaga Lake, raised $310,000 toward a completely new museum complex. In 1987, the Onondaga County Legislature authorized a bond issue of $1,200,000. The National Endowment for the Humanities awarded a $175,000 grant for special exhibits. New York State awarded $700,000 through its 1986 Environmental Bond Act. Federal and state grants made up the balance for the $2,570,000 cost.

Acting as project liaison between the County and the Onondaga Indian Nation in developing the exhibits on the Iroquois was Richard Hill. As an Iroquois, and a consultant to the New York State and Canadian Governments, he was special assistant to the Director of the National Museum of the American Indian Smithsonian Institution. Other scholars from both Canada and the United States employed as consultants included Dr. James Bradley, Archeologist, Commonwealth of Massachusetts, Survey Director; Dr. Pierre Dufour, Historian; Minnie Garrow, Mohawk; Dr. Conrad Heidenreich, Cultural Geographer, York University, Ontario; Barry Powless, Onondaga, educator; Dr. Daniel Richter, Dickinson College; Dr. Laurier Turgeon, Universite Laval, Montreal. Other contributors were Rev. Adrien Pouliot, S. J. of Quebec and M. Andre Desrosiers, archivist at the Public Archives of Canada .

Part II: History of Sainte Marie

Introduction

The building of the Jesuit mission *Sainte Marie among the Iroquois* on Onondaga Lake in the middle of the 17th century was the first European settlement in the territory of the Iroquois in what is now central New York. It is the only historic French site of that period in the United States.

After Columbus found land and treasure for Spain at the end of the 15th century, other European countries launched similar ventures. In 1534, the French sent Jacques Cartier to the northeastern part of the North American continent in search of gold and silver, as well as a new route to the East.

At that time most of the 16,000,000 French were subsisting on a hand-to-mouth existence, struggling for survival. A series of civil and religious wars had left most of the common people frightened, hungry, dirty, victims of marauding soldiers, and dying early from disease epidemics. They were subjected to heavy taxes imposed to support the King and his nobles in a lavish lifestyle. They had few rights or privileges.

Origin of Term "Indian"

On the other side of the Atlantic Ocean was a continent with a largely unknown population estimated by some at eighteen million in North America. Each of the many tribes had a separate language and culture. (Dobyns, 343) Yet, the Europeans came to refer to all as "Indians." The term arose from the name Europeans used for all of Asia east of the river Indus - India. (Berkhofer, 5) Columbus, supposing he had landed in the East, thus called the people he met "los Indios." The Spanish continued to use the term to refer to all the peoples of the Americas. From the Spanish term came the French "Indien," the German "Indianer," the English "Indian." The term has persisted. (Berkhofer, 3, 5)

11

French Found Quebec

It was not until 1608 that Champlain established a permanent French settlement at what is now Quebec. He formed alliances with the Montaignais, the Algonquins, and the Hurons who lived north of the St. Lawrence River Valley. These tribes were often at war with those nations occupying what is now central New York - the Ho-de-no-sau-nee - meaning People of the Longhouse. From east to west they were the Mohawks, then the Oneida, the Onondaga, the Cayuga, and the Seneca. United in a powerful political organization known as the Iroquois Confederacy, they formed an alliance first with the Dutch, and later the English. The Iroquois warriors were able to extend their influence far beyond their borders.

Early French explorers, Jacques Cartier and Samuel de Champlain, kept journals as they traveled inland. They wrote detailed descriptions of the natural environment, as well as, their interaction with the Native Americans.

Jesuit Journals

French Jesuits, members of a Catholic religious order named the Society of Jesus, wrote daily reports of their experiences. As missionaries carrying the word of Christ to the Native Americans, they lived in the villages. Most learned the languages and shared the lifestyle.

These reports present their observations of life at this early time. They contain graphic accounts of daily living, they often quoted the speeches, described the ceremonies, and noted the political actions of the Native Americans in their meetings with the French. Published annually in Paris, their reports came to be known as the "Jesuit Relations."

Pierre Radisson

A young French adventurer, Pierre Radisson, wrote a vivid account of his experiences at Sainte Marie. Born in St. Malo, France, he emigrated to Canada with his family in 1651. With his brother-in-law he made many long journeys across Canada to the Far West in fur-trading expeditions from 1652 to 1664.

From careful notes made during his wanderings he wrote a narrative during a voyage to England in 1665. The manuscripts are preserved in the archives of the Bodleian Library at Oxford University and the British Museum.

These sources are not widely available. The following eyewitness excerpts have been selected to highlight the events in the establishment of *Sainte Marie Among the Iroquois*. The reader can step back in time, retrace the steps of these early writers, share with them the customs, beliefs, and lifestyle of both French and Iroquois at this early time and, thereby, enhance a visit to *Sainte Marie among the Iroquois*.

Iroquois round bark hut used temporarily for hunting and fishing expeditions erected at *Sainte Marie.*

1

The French Send Cartier

For a short time in the middle of the 17th Century a few Frenchmen lived among the Iroquois in what is now Central New York. After opening the Jesuit mission *Sainte Marie* on the shores of Onondaga Lake in the summer of 1656, the fifty-three French abruptly departed during the night of March 20, 1658.

The story of that mission comes to life in the eyewitness accounts of the Jesuits and other French as they traveled to the land of the Onondagas. Carefully, they noted the animals and fish, as well as the plants and trees while crossing the rivers and lakes. However, most important of all, they described their experiences living among the Iroquois at the beginning of close contact.

The history begins when the King of France sent Jacques Cartier in 1534 to the northeastern part of North America in search of gold and silver for France and a new route to the East.

From fishing voyages to the Grand Banks off Newfoundland in earlier years, Cartier had become interested in going further inland. In a letter to the High Admiral of France he proposed an official voyage to the American coast. The King approved an expedition of two ships of sixty tons each with a crew of sixty-one (Burrage, 3).

Cartier, or one of his companions, wrote a detailed journal of the voyage. It began as follows: "After Sir Charles de Mouy of La Mailleraye and Vice-Admiral of France had sworn the captains, mates, and sailors of the ships to be well and faithfully true to the service of His Christian Majesty the King, under the authority and charge of Jacques Cartier, we set sail, the twentieth of April, 1534, from St. Malo" (Cartier 1890,11).

Arriving in Newfoundland 10 May, they spent two months exploring the rugged coast to find an inland passage. Several times they saw Native Americans on the shore and sometimes talked and traded with them. While they were riding out a storm in July, they anchored for a week in a sheltered harbor:

> We saw a large number who were mackerel fishing, which are very plentiful; there were about forty canoes of them, and more than two hundred men, women and children, who, after meeting us on shore came familiarly to our ships with their canoes. We gave them knives, glass chaplets [beads], combs and other articles . . . which greatly pleased them (Cartier 1890, 29,30).

> On 24 July, we made a large cross, thirty feet high; this was made in the presence of some of them at the point at the entrance of the harbor [Gaspe]; on the middle of which cross we put a shield in relief with three fleur-de-lys, above which we cut out in large letters "Vive le Roy de France," and we erected it in their presence on the point, and they looked at it keenly, both when we were making it and while erecting it. . . . we all joined hands and knelt down in adoration of it before their eyes, and we made signs to them, looking and pointing to heaven, that in this was our salvation. This astonished them greatly; they turned to each other and looked at the cross.

> Having gone back to our ships, their captain came to us in a canoe with three of his sons and a brother; they did not come as close as usual. The chief made a long speech, pointing to the cross and making a representation of it with his two fingers. Then he pointed to the district round us, as if to say it was all his, and we should not have erected the cross without his permission.

> Having finished, we showed him a hatchet, as if we wished to exchange it for his bearskin . . .and he gradually came close to our ships.

Cartier Abducts two Indians

One of our sailors, who was in the ship's boat, laid his hand on the canoe, and instantly jumped into it with two or three more, and obliged them to go on board ship, at

15

which they were much astonished. But our Captain at once assured them they would receive no hurt, making signs of friendship to them, welcoming them to eat and drink.

After this, we gave them to understand by signs that the cross was placed there as a guide and mark to enter the harbor, and that we wished to return here shortly and that we would bring iron tools and other things, and that we wished to take with us two of his sons and that we would return again to this harbor.

And we dressed each of the sons in a shift, a colored sack [waist], and a red cape, and we placed a brass chain around the neck of each, which pleased them immensely. They gave their old clothes to those who returned. We gave a hatchet and some knives to each one of the three we sent back.

When they reached shore, they related what had passed to the others. About noontime, six of their canoes, with five or six men in each, came to the ships, bringing fish to the chief's sons [Taignoagny and Domagaya]. The men bid them adieu, and said some words to them which we could not understand. They made signs that they would not remove the cross (Cartier 1890,31-33).

Cartier continued exploring among the bays, capes, and islands, describing each in detail and naming them. He noted the latitude and longitude, distances in leagues from one to the other, and depths in fathoms. Departing on 15 August, he arrived back at St. Malo on 5 September (Cartier 1890, 37).

Cartier presented his two young guests to the King and made a report of his voyage. As a result, he received a new commission. As "Captain and Pilot of the King," he was given three vessels, well equipped and furnished with enough provisions for 15 months (Cartier 1890, 35,37).

The next spring, on 19 May, Cartier set sail again from St. Malo with "Grand Hermine," 120 tons, "Petite Hermine," 60 tons and "Emerillon," 40 tons. Having learned some of the French

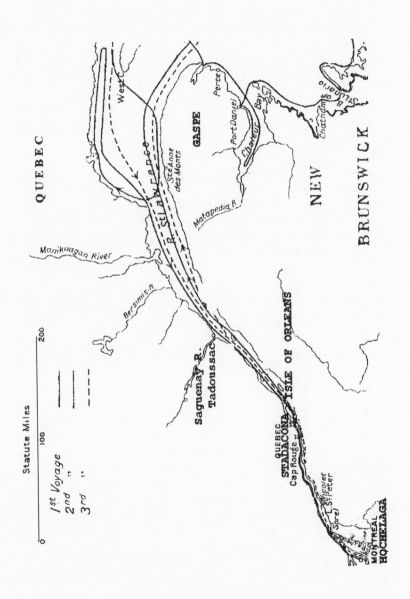

Voyages of Jacques Cartier

17

Language, the two Native Americans became his guides and interpreters as he explored further (Cartier 1890, 42.

Cartier Finds the St. Lawrence River
After a stormy voyage, the three ships met at Newfoundland, and, on 29 July, set off to find the passage to the inland river. On 12 August, the two Native Americans recognized familiar territory:

> the way or road to go to Honguedo [Gaspé], where we had seized them in our voyage, the year previous. They also told us that two days' journey from the said cape and island commenced the country and kingdom of Saguenay, on the land to the north leading to Canada . . . [They] informed us that this was the river and commencement of the grand "Sileune de Hockelaga" and river of Canada [St. Lawrence]; which river grows narrower going towards Canada, where it was fresh, and came from so far off that no one had ever reached its source that our Indians had ever heard tell of; and, of course, only boats could be used as a means of passage (Cartier 1890, 44,45).

For several days they proceeded up the river:

> Anchoring between this island [Isle of Orleans] and the north bank, we went ashore, taking with us the two [Indians] we had secured the preceding voyage. We found there several of the . . .people, who took to flight and would not come near until our two men began to talk to them, telling them that they were Taignoagny and Domagaya. As soon as they were satisfied of this, they showed their joy, dancing and performing antics, and came to speak to us at the boats, bringing eels and other fish, with two or three loads of large grain [corn], which is the bread on which they live, and several large melons [probably pumpkins].

18

The same day several canoes of Indians, male and female, came to our ships to see and welcome our two Indians, all of whom were well received by our captain, who feasted them as well as he could.

The next day, the seigneur of Canada, his name being Donnacona and his title Agouhanna, came with twelve canoes, and, leaving ten behind as he came near the ships, approached us with only two, accompanied by sixteen men, and made a speech . . . of joy and welcome (Cartier 1890, 49,50).

Cartier Anchors at Stadacona (Quebec)

Then, coming to the Captain's ship he spoke with the young men and heard about their time in France. When the tide turned, Cartier ordered the boats higher in the river for a safer harbor. Nearby was the village of Donnacona called Stadacona [Quebec].

Next day, the fifteenth, our Captain went ashore to place buoys to ensure the safety of our ships, to which place came several of the native people, amongst others Donnacona, our two and their band, but these all kept apart from us on the border of a stream, none of them approaching us.

As Cartier prepared to explore further on the river he found Donnacona very opposed. Taignoagny and Domagaya told the captain that Donnacona was unwilling that any of them should go with the captain to Hochelaga. The captain told them they could remain behind and "that he would not be prevented from going" (Cartier 1890, 56,57).

On 19 September, Cartier advanced up the St. Lawrence with his pinnace, "Emerillon," two boats, and a company of fifty men. Along the way they found friendly Indians who brought them fish and other food (Cartier 1890, 57).

Cartier Describes the St. Lawrence

From the nineteenth to the twenty-eighth we had been sailing up the river without losing an hour, during which time we saw as fine a country and soil as could be wished for, full of fine trees, such as oak, elm, walnut, cedar, spruce, ash, osiers, birch, willows, and plenty of vines, which vines were so loaded with grapes that our sailors came on board with all they could carry.

There are large numbers of cranes, swans, outards, geese, plover, pheasants, partridges [grouse], blackbirds, thrushes, doves, goldfinches, canaries, nightingales, and other birds (Cartier 1890, 58).

Fish of all kinds abound in the river; nearly all kinds of salt and fresh water fish; also will be found in Canada large numbers of whales, cod, sea-horses, and adhothuys, a kind of fish we had never seen or heard of. They are as large as a cod, white as snow, have a body and head like a greyhound and stay in brackish water between the river of Saguenay and Canada. There will also be found in June, July and August plenty of mackerel, mullet, barr, large eels, and plenty of lampreys and salmon. In Canada are bass, trout, carp, bream, and other fresh water fish. And all the fish are taken in large numbers by the tribes for food (Cartier 1890, 76).

Cartier Visits Hochelaga (Montreal)

On 29 September, it was too shallow to proceed with the pinnace, so Cartier took the two boats the rest of the way to Hochelaga with four nobles and twenty-eight sailors. The others stayed with the "Emerillon."

Three days later there came to meet us above a thousand persons, men, women and children . . . the men danced in a group together, the women in another, and the children in another showing great joy . . . they brought us a great number of fish and much of their bread, made with large grain [corn], which they threw

20

into our boats in such quantities that it seemed to be falling from the air. Our captain, seeing this, went ashore with several others. As soon as he had landed, they all gathered round him and the others, welcoming them warmly; and they brought their children in their arms to touch the captain and others . . . Our captain, seeing their good-will caused the women to sit down in rows and gave them tin bells and such trifles, and, to some of the men, he gave knives. Then he returned to the boats to sup and pass the night

Next day the captain put on his regimentals [military uniform] and put his men in proper order to go and see the town and dwelling place of this tribe, and the mountain adjacent to the town. With the captain went the nobles and twenty sailors; he left the rest to guard the boats. Three men of the said town of Hochelaga led the way to it.

We found the road a well-beaten one and as fine a soil as one could wish to see, filled with oaks as fine as in the forests of France, the ground underneath which trees was covered with acorns. Having walked about a league and a half we met one of the chiefs of the town, accompanied by several men, which chief made us stop at the fire he had made on the road, which we did, and then he made a long speech, as is their custom, showing joy and friendship, and greeted our captain and his associates warmly (Cartier 1890, 61).

This is an ancient ritual of the Iroquois League, a tradition known as the so-called Welcome at the Woods' Edge and was described subsequently when the Jesuits noted their reception at the villages of the Iroquois (Woodbury,xi).

The captain gave him a couple of axes, knives and a crucifix, which he made him kiss and hang it round his neck; at which the captain was thanked.

21

Cartier Names "le Mont Royal"

We marched further, and about half a league further from there, we began to see ploughed land and large fields of their wheat, . . . and amidst these fields is situated the town of Hochelaga, near to and touching a mountain, which is around it, very fertile and cultivated and from the summit of which one can see far off. We called this mountain "le Mont Royal" (Cartier 1890,61).

The town is round in shape and enclosed with three rows of timbers in the shape of a pyramid crossed on top, having the middle stakes perpendicular, and the others at an angle on each side, well joined and fastened in their fashion. It is of the height of two lances and there is only one entrance through a gate which can be barred.

There were in the town about fifty houses, each fifty steps or more in length and twelve or fifteen wide, all made of wood covered with bark and strips of wood as large as a table, sewn well together artificially in their way; within, there were several rooms.

In the centre of the house there was a large space used as a fireplace, where they eat in common, each man retiring afterwards to his rooms with his wife and children. Likewise they have lofts or granaries in their houses, where they store their corn, out of which they make their bread, which they call "Carraconny."

Baking Indian Bread

The following is their method of making it. They have mortars of wood similar to those used for making hemp, and they pound the corn into flour [en pouldre], then gather it into dough, make it into cakes, which they place upon a large hot rock, then cover it with hot stones; and thus they bake their bread instead of in an oven. They have large vessels in their houses, like casks, in which they place their fish, which they smoke during the summer and eat during the winter; and of these they lay in big stores, as we know by experience. All their food is eaten without a taste of salt. They sleep on bark, spread on the ground with . . . skins of animals, of which they also make their clothes, such as squirrels, beavers, martens, foxes, lynxes, deer and others (Cartier 1890, 62).

We were conducted by our guides to the centre of the town, where there is an open space about a stone's throw square; and there, they made us signs to come to a halt . . . suddenly, gathered the women and children who made signs to us - it would please them if we would touch their infants.

After this the women withdrew and the men sat down on the ground around us. Several women brought square mats and made us sit down on them . . . their king and chief, whom they call Agouhanna, was carried in by nine or ten men, seated on a large deerskin and they placed him on mats near our captain. He was about fifty years of age, no better dressed than the others, except that he had a red crown on his head, made out of the skin of a hedge-hog. All his limbs were disabled.

Having saluted our captain, welcoming us, he showed his arms and limbs to the captain making signs that he would be pleased to have him touch them and the captain rubbed them with his hands; and immediately were brought to the captain several sick people - blind, lame, those with only one eye, cripples, etc.; setting and laying themselves down near our captain, so that he might touch them; as if they thought God had sent him to cure them.

Our captain, seeing their simplicity and faith, read the Gospel of St. John and making the sign of the cross over the sick, prayed to God to give them knowledge of our holy faith, and grace to receive Christianity and Baptism (Cartier 1890, 64,65).

After reading from the Bible the captain distributed hatchets, knives, beads and small rings etc.

23

Then, he ordered the trumpets and other musical instruments to be sounded at which they were astounded. Then taking our leave, we went out. . . . After we were outside the town, several men and women came to lead us up the mountain, which we had named Mont Royal, distant about a quarter of a league. Having reached the summit, we could see more than thirty leagues round about.

View from Mont Royal

Towards the north, a range of mountains, lying east and west and also one to the south. Between these ranges the soil is fertile, level, and easy of cultivation, and in the middle of the plain we could see the river further than the place where our boats were; also a rapid as impetuous as possible, impossible of ascent by us, though we saw it was large and deep beyond this, going towards the southwest, and passing three round mountains, which we could see, and estimated to be distant about fifteen leagues from us. Those who had guided us made signs that there were three rapids in the river, but we could not make out how far distant, as we could not speak to them.

. . . We returned to our boats, attended by a large number of these people, . . . Our departure caused these people great regret; they followed us as long as they could along the river (Cartier 1890, 65-67).

Monday, the eleventh October we arrived at the river St. Croix, where were our ships and found our mates and sailors who had remained behind. They had made a fort in front of the ships out of large pieces of timber placed perpendicularly side by side, guns at all points, in a good condition of defence against the power of the whole country (Cartier 1890, 67,68).

Winter on the St. Lawrence

From the middle of November till the fifteenth of April we were continuously shut in by the ice which was more than two fathoms thick. On the ground there was more that four feet of snow, being higher than the sides of our ships, for the same period of time. Our drinkables were frozen in their casks; the ice was four inches thick on the hull and rigging and all the river, being fresh water up to Hochelaga, was also frozen.

During this time we lost by death twenty-five souls, all good men and now there were not more than fifty whom we considered strong and vigorous; the remainder all sick, with the exception of three or four who were free altogether (Cartier 1890,80).

Epidemic of Scurvy

In the month of December we became aware that death was visiting the tribe of Stadacona to so great a degree that already more than fifty had passed away, for which reason we forbade them coming to our fort or amongst us. In spite of this we were sorely visited with the epidemic, unknown and mysterious to us [scurvy]; the sick lost flesh and their legs became swollen, muscles contracted and black as coal; covered with purple blood blisters. Then the disease affected the thighs and shoulders, arms and neck. In each instance, the mouth was so diseased that the flesh fell off, even to the roots of the teeth, and nearly all the teeth fell out. And so much did the sickness prevail amongst us that, in February, out of one hundred and ten souls that we had been, not ten were free from it; and one could not assist another (Cartier 1890, 77-8).

One day the captain, seeing the sickness so prevalent, and his men so overcome by it, being outside the fort and walking on the ice, saw a band of the people of Stadacona approaching, in which was Domagaya, whom the captain had seen very ill with the disease ten or twelve days previously. He had then one of his knees

25

swollen to the size of a child of two years; all his muscles contracted; his teeth had fallen out and his jaws had been mortified and diseased.

Cure for Scurvy

Our captain, seeing Domagaya healthy and well, was overjoyed . . . When they had come near the fort, the captain asked him how he had been cured. Domagaya replied he had taken the juice and grounds of the leaves of a tree, which had cured him, and this was the peculiar remedy for the malady and asked if there was any of the remedy thereabouts, as he wished to cure his servant (valet) , . . not wishing to let him know how many of his men were sick.

Then Domagaya sent two women to get some; they brought nine or ten branches and showed us how to take off the bark and leaves and to put all to boil in water, then to drink of it for two days and put the grounds on the swollen limbs. This tree, they said, cured all diseases; they call the tree in their language "ameda" (Cartier 1890, 81).

The ameda or annedda, the arbor vitae and Thuja occidentalis were, and are, one and the same tree. A study of extract taken from bark and needles of conifers showed the presence of ascorbic acid, vitamin C, which cured the disease scurvy. Cartier thus benefited from the herbal medical knowledge of the Native Americans at this early time. Not until 1932 was Vitamin C isolated in fresh vegetables and fruit by the research of C. G. King and W. A. Waugh. It was also found that a Thuja occidentalis or arbor vitae was brought to the Royal Garden of Fontainebleau in France around either 1536 or 1542 (Cartier 1953,128,129).

A tree as large as an oak in France, was consumed in six days, which produced an effect that had all the doctors of Lourain and Montpellyer been present, with all the drugs of Alexandria, they could not have affected as

26

much in a year as this tree did in six days, for it was so beneficial that all those who were willing to use it were cured and recovered their health (Cartier 1890, 82).

The captain was determined to take the Chief Donnacona back to France to relate to the King the wonders of the world he had seen in the western countries. He had assured us he had been in the Saguenay kingdom, where are infinite gold, rubies, and other riches; and there are white men there as in France and dressed in woollen clothing . . . This chief, Donnacona, is an old man, and had travelled, as long as he could remember, through countries, across rivers, streams and by land.

Cartier Erects Cross for France

The third of May, the fete of the Holy Cross, the captain had a cross erected, about thirty-five feet high, under the crossbar of which there was a shield of wood of the arms of France and on it written "FRANCISCUS PRIMUS DEI GRATIA FRANCORUM REGNAT" [Francis I, by the grace of God, King of France].

About noon came men, women and children to say that Donnacona, Taignoagny, Domagaia and others were coming, which gave us much satisfaction, as we hoped to seize them. They came about two o'clock; and when they had come down to the ships, our captain went to greet Donnacona, who warmly received him, but kept his eye on the forest and was in great fear. Then came Taignoagny, who told Donnacona not to enter the fort. . . . The captain invited him to come and eat on board ship, as customary. He likewise asked Taignoagny, who said he would go by and by. They entered the fort.

Cartier Abducts Indians to Take to France

Taignoagny came in to bring him out. Our captain seeing there was no other way, gave the order to seize them. . . . The Canadians, seeing the capture, began to run and flee like sheep before the wolf, some across the river, others into the forest, each one looking out for his

27

own safety. The capture effected, and the others having fled, the captives were put in a secure place (Cartier 1890, 84-6).

All night the people came down to the ships in large numbers, calling to speak to the captives. At noon the next day, our captain gave orders to put the chief in an elevated position that he might speak to his people as follows:

The captain told him he would be well-treated, that after he had related to the King of France what he had seen in the Saguenay and other places he could return in ten or twelve months and that the King would make him a grand present, which pleased Donnacona greatly and he told his people, who gave three wonderful cries, in token of joy. Donnacona and his people made speeches to each other, which we could not understand, as we did not know the language.

Our captain told Donnacona to have some of his people come on board as they could talk better together, and that they would be safe. Donnacona did so, and a boatload of them came on board. They renewed their talks, praising our captain, and presented him with twenty-four strings of wampum, which is their most precious possession, valuing it more than gold or silver.

Having talked enough and seeing there was no escape and that he was obliged to go to France, Donnacona ordered them to bring him food for his voyage. Our captain presented him with two brass fry pans or buckets, hatchets, knives, beads and other trifles which pleased him. He sent them to his wives and children. The captain also gave presents to those who had come to talk to Donnacona, for which they were grateful. They then left and went back to their homes (Cartier 1890, 87-8).

On the fifth of May a very large number came to the shore. A boat with four women brought a large quantity of corn, meat, fish and other kinds of their food. Providing food was the task of the women in their culture. The Captain assured them he would return Donnacona in twelve months (Cartier 1890, 88).

The expedition proceeded down the St. Lawrence, but was delayed many days along the way waiting for favorable winds. Finally leaving the coast of America on 19 June, they arrived at St. Malo 6 July 1536. The change of climate and way of living, as well as exposure to European diseases proved unhealthy for those they captured, and all died, except one young girl (Cartier 1890, 91,95).

Cartier Returns

Cartier did not make his next voyage until 23 May, 1540, when he set out with five ships to explore further and attain knowledge of the country of the Saguenay where there were great riches, according to Donnacona. The ships were furnished with provisions for two years. They carried cattle, as well as goats, hogs and other beasts.

However, contrary winds forced a long voyage of three months. They did not arrive at their former port on the St. Lawrence until 23 August. They were met by Agona, who had replaced Donnacona as chief. He inquired of the captain where Donnacona and the rest were. The Captain answered that Donnacona was dead in France and that his body rested in the earth. He lied that the rest stayed there as great lords, and were married, and would not return back unto their country (Cartier 1890, 97,101,102).

Cartier preferred to winter his vessels further up the river at Cap Rouge. On a high and steep cliff, he built a fort. He sent back to France two of his vessels with the news of his finds and then explored further up the river to see the rapids and falls. The account of this voyage is incomplete. However, it is known that Cartier returned to France and ended his explorations.

2

Champlain Founds New France

Fishermen and explorers continued to visit the northeastern coast of America during the rest of the century, as they had from an unknown time. However, the French did not attempt another expedition to explore along the St. Lawrence until the beginning of the 17th century. Europe had become embroiled in decades of war, killing hundreds of thousands in the name of religion following the posting of Martin Luther's 95 theses in 1517.

At the end of the century a peace agreement brought Henry IV to the throne of France as head of a Catholic country and the Huguenots (Protestants) were granted limited freedom of religious beliefs. With peace came reform. Agriculture, trade and manufacturing were encouraged.

Trade between Europeans and Native Americans had been limited until the beaver hat became fashionable in Europe. During the last quarter of the sixteenth century gentleman in the courts of kings began to wear a hat of beaver felt. It was this fashion that sent traders across the sea and Indians to the beaver ponds to capture the animals.

Beaver Hat

As the demand for beaver pelts rose, the small and local Indian groups along the shores quickly hunted out the beaver populations nearby to exchange furs for European trade goods. This trade then expanded inland along previously established routes.

At the beginning of the seventeenth century French traders were obtaining increasing supplies of furs from the Montagnais at Tadoussac, the junction of the Saguenay River and the St. Lawrence. However, the English began to raid the returning French vessels and take them to English ports. The French needed a fortified colony to protect its source of supply and lines of communication (Bishop,34).

After several attempts to establish a settlement, King Henry IV authorized a fact-finding expedition of three ships in 1603. Samuel de Champlain was an observer and cartographer on this first of several voyages to what became New France. Francois Gravé, Sieur du Pont, was the captain. Two young Montagnais Indians, the Captain had taken to France on a previous voyage, acted as interpreters and ambassadors of good will (Bishop,36,38,39).

Champlain Attends Tabagie

After a two-month stormy voyage across the Atlantic, they reached Cape Gaspé and started up the St. Lawrence. Champlain reported in his journal on 24 May:

> we cast anchor before Tadoussac, and on the twenty-sixth entered the harbor, which is like a cove at the mouth of the Saguenay river. . . On the twenty-seventh, accompanied by the two Indians [taken to France on a previous voyage and now returned] whom Monsieur du Pont brought to make report of what they had seen in France and of the good reception the King had given them, we sought the Indians at St. Matthew's point, which is a league from Tadoussac.
>
> As soon as we landed, we went to the lodge of their grand Sagamore, a man named Anadabijou where we found him and some eighty or one hundred of his companions, making *Tabagie* (that is to say, a feast). He received us very well, after the fashion of the country, and made us sit down beside him, while all the Indians ranged themselves one next the other on both sides of the lodge.

31

One of the two Indians whom we had brought began to make his oration, of the good reception that the king had given them and of the good entertainment they had received in France, and that they might feel assured His Majesty wished them well, and desired to people their country, and to make peace with their enemies (who are the Iroquois) or send forces to vanquish them. He also told of the fine castles, palaces, houses and peoples they had seen and our manner of living. He was heard with the greatest possible silence.

When he had finished his oration, the said Grand Sagamore Anadabijou, who had listened to him attentively, began to smoke tobacco, and to pass his pipe to Monsieur du Pont-Grave' of St. Malo and to me, and to certain other Sagamores who were near him. After smoking some time, he began to address the whole gathering, speaking with gravity, pausing sometimes a little, and then resuming his speech, saying to them, that in truth they ought to be very glad to have His Majesty for their great friend. They answered all with one voice, *Ho, ho, ho,* which is say, *yes, yes.*

Continuing his speech, he said that he was well content that His said Majesty should people their country, and make war on their enemies, and that there was no nation in the world to which they wished more good than to the French (Champlain 1922, 98-101).

The St. Lawrence Valley had become a war zone. The alliance of the French with the Algonquins, Montagnais and Hurons against the powerful Iroquois and their Dutch (later their English) allies, began at this tabagie. The French would be considered friends and allowed to settle among them. Each side was looking for military allies as well as trading partners (Ray and Freeman,19-23; Bishop,45, 46)

Champlain Describes Canoes

On 28 May the Grand Sagamo went to the lodges and cried out that:

they should break camp to go to Tadoussac where their good friends were. Immediately every man in a trice took down his lodge, and the said grand Captain was the first to begin to take his canoe and carry it to the water, wherein he embarked his wife and children and a quantity of furs; and in like manner were launched well nigh two hundred canoes, which go extraordinarily well; for though our shallop was well-manned, yet they went more swiftly than we. There are but two that paddle, the man and his wife. Their canoes are some eight or nine paces long, and a pace or a pace and a half broad amidships, and grow sharper and sharper toward both ends. They are very liable to overturn, if one know not how to manage them rightly; for they are made of a bark of trees called birch-bark, strengthened within by little curcles of wood strongly and neatly fashioned, and are so light that a man can carry one of them easily; and every canoe can carry the weight of a pipe [about 1,000 pounds applied to wine] (Champlain 1922, 104, 105).

Exploring on the St. Lawrence, Champlain made careful notes on landmarks, the channel, dangers to navigation, the soil, plants, etc. The Huron town of Hochelaga visited by Cartier had disappeared.

On 16 August they set sail for home carrying extra passengers - an Iroquois woman and the son of a Montagnais Sagamore, Bechourat. On the recommendation of the Sagamore Anadabijou, the Chief wanted his son "to see everything the other two had seen" (Champlain 1922,188).

Champlain reported to the King that the country was most fit for colonization and for profitable fur trading. He was also convinced that not far to the west lay the South Sea and access to all the wealth of the East (Champlain 1971,100; Bishop,54-5).

To the delight of the three-year-old French Prince, Dauphin Louis, the young son of the Montagnais chief was baptized, dressed in a blue coat and bonnet, and lodged in the palace of Saint-Germain. However, he became ill through the winter and died in June 1604 (Bishop, 56).

After making two more voyages exploring the North Atlantic coast, Champlain opened a trading post and fort in 1608 for the French. His "Habitation" stood approximately on the site of the present church of Notre-Dame des Victoires (Bishop, 128; Champlain 1907,131).

Champlain agrees to meet the Iroquois

To insure friendly relations with the nearby Algonquins and Hurons Champlain agreed to accompany a war-party against their traditional enemies, the Mohawks, one of the five Iroquois Nations (Bishop, 141,142).

Before the arrival of Europeans, the League of the Iroquois was founded to end years of war and bring peace to the Mohawks, the Oneidas, the Onondagas, the Cayugas, and the Senecas - the five nations of the Iroquois.

The Confederacy provided a ritual to redress grievances or injury, to prevent vendettas or violence between members as well as secure cooperation and support. "It was transmitted orally from one generation to the next through certain lords or sachems of the confederacy who had made it their business to learn it" (Fenton, 7). Beginning in 1880 a written record was compiled (Fenton 39-46).

League of the Iroquois

The establishment of the Great Peace by the Peacemaker is attributed according to the prefatory articles of the Great Immutable Law:

I am Dekanawideh and with the Five Nations' confederate lords I plant the Tree of the Great Peace. I plant it in your territory, Adodarhoh and the Onondaga Nation, in the territory of you who are the fire keepers. .

I, Dekanawideh, and the confederate lords now uproot the tallest pine tree and into the cavity thereby made, we cast all weapons of war. Into the depths of the earth, down into the deep underearth currents of water flowing into unknown regions, we cast all weapons of strife. We bury them from sight forever and plant again

34

the tree. Thus shall all Peace be established and hostilities shall no longer be known between the Five Nations but only peace to a united people (Fenton 1968, 8,9).

The tribes of each nation were divided with one-fifth being placed in each of the five nations. This action preserves a tie of brotherhood between the separated parts. It also links the nations together with indissoluble bonds. In the eyes of an Iroquois, every member of his own tribe, in whatever nation, was as much his brother or his sister as if children of the same mother (Morgan, 77).

The League was effective in uniting the five tribes and settling differences between them. However, it was necessary for them to come to a unanimous decision on cooperative action against outside tribes. This provision was to cause them difficulty as they dealt with the colonies of competing European nations.

Champlain Joins Warparty

As Champlain was particularly interested in learning more about the country and its people, he accompanied his allies as they gathered to make war on the Mohawks. Leaving Quebec after the traditional five days of feasting and dancing, the warparty ascended the St. Lawrence and then the Richelieu River until they reached the rapids of Chambly. Champlain sent his shallop back to Quebec as it was too large to navigate the rapids. He proceeded in one of the twenty-four canoes with sixty Hurons, Montagnais and Ottawa Algonquins.

At ten o'clock on the evening of 29 July they came to a cape on the westward shore of what is now Lake Champlain (probably Crown Point). Out of the dark came loud shouts and cries. It was a warparty of Mohawk Iroquois heading north in their elm-bark canoes. The invaders lay off the shore, tying their canoes together with long poles.

Warriors in two Iroquois canoes paddled out for a parley with the enemy "to inquire if they wished to fight, to which the latter replied that they wanted nothing else."

Champlain's drawing of the Defeat of the Iroquois at Lake Champlain 1609, from <u>Les Voyages</u> (1613) Courtesy of Library of Congress. A. The Fort of the Iroquois. B. The enemy. C. The enemy's canoes made of oak-bark (actually elm) and each capable of holding 10, 15, and 18 men. D.E. Two Chiefs killed and one wounded by a shot from Champlains's arquebus. F. Champlain. G. Two arquebusiers. H. Montagnais, Hurons and Algonquins. I. Canoes of our Indian allies made of birch-bark. K. The woods. (Letters A.G.K. are missing.)

As there was not much light, it would be necessary to wait for daylight, so as to be able to recognize each other; and that as soon as the sun rose, they would offer us battle. This was agreed by our side. (Champlain 1907, 163-164).

The etiquette of warfare decreed a parley, an hour for battle and even extended to letting the enemy go ashore unhindered at dawn.

Champlain described the action as follows:

> After this singing, dancing, and bandying words on both sides to the fill, when day came, my companions and myself continued under cover, for fear that the enemy would see us. We arranged our arms in the best manner possible, being however, separated, each in one of the canoes of the Montagnais. After arming ourselves with light armor, we each took an arquebus, and went on shore.
>
> I saw the enemy go out of their barricade, nearly two hundred in number, stout and rugged in appearance. They came at a slow pace towards us, with a dignity and assurance with greatly pleased me, having three chiefs at their head. Our men also advanced in the same order, telling me that those who had three large plumes were the chiefs . . . and that I should do what I could to kill them. I promised to do all in my power.
>
> As soon as we had landed, they began to run for some two hundred paces towards their enemies, who stood firmly, not having noticed my companions, who went into the woods. . . Our men began to call me with loud cries; and in order to give me a passage-way, they opened in two parts, and put me at their head, where I marched some twenty paces in advance of the rest, until I was within thirty paces of the enemy, who at once noticed me, and halting, gazed at me, as I did also at them.
>
> When I saw them making a move to fire at us, I rested my musket against my cheek, and aimed directly at one of the three chiefs. With the same shot, two fell to the ground; one of their men was so wounded that he died some time after. I had loaded my musket with four balls.

When our side saw this shot so favorable for them, they began to raise such loud cries that one could not have heard it thunder. Meanwhile the arrows flew on both sides. The Iroquois were greatly astonished that two men had been so quickly killed, although they were equipped with armor woven from cotton [?] thread, and with wood which was proof against their arrows. This caused great alarm among them. As I was loading again, one of my companions fired a shot from the woods, which astonished them anew to such a degree that, seeing their chiefs dead, they lost courage, and took to flight, abandoning their camp and fort, and fleeing into the woods. Our Indians also killed several and took ten or twelve prisoners. The remainder escaped with the wounded. Fifteen or sixteen were wounded on our side with arrow shots, but they were soon healed (Champlain 1907, 164-65).

The defeat of the Iroquois in this action 30 July 1609 made the Algonquins and their allies, the Montagnais and Hurons, lasting friends of the French. However, it was the beginning of a usually hostile relation between the French and the Mohawks.

Voyage of Henry Hudson same year

By coincidence, a few weeks later that summer Henry Hudson, representing the Dutch, approached the same area as he sailed up the river to be named for him.

In subsequent years Dutch traders followed Hudson along the Hudson River. By 1614 they had established a trading post on Castle Island near what is now Albany. Later, after it was flooded, Fort Orange was built by the Dutch West India Company. The defeated Mohawks thus become allies of the Dutch and found their source for guns.

The demand for furs in Europe sparked the rise of competing English, French and Dutch trading companies eager to make their fortunes.

As for the Iroquois, they welcomed the trade goods. Many gave up the heavy clay pots for lighter metal ones to cook. They exchanged stones for sharp metal knives to skin hides.

Instead of using a whole sapling for building, they began to use an axe to cut trees or chop wood, and to use a saw to cut planks.

Without sheep for wool, without flax for linen, without a warm climate to grow cotton, they had no cloth. Thus, the women began to make garments of cloth brought by the traders. They began to sew with a metal needle instead of the usual bone.

By paying well in trade goods, the Dutch encouraged the Iroquois warriors to bring them furs from the cold north as they were of superior quality. Thus, Iroquois raiders were increasingly active and bold in attacking the Hurons and taking the pelts they had secured from distant tribes. Huron losses in men and goods were increasing and it followed that the losses affected the French as well.

The Huron and Algonquin desired to strike the enemy in his own country and had asked Champlain to give them aid (Bishop,214).

Champlain agreed to accompany a warparty against the Iroquois in 1615. The friendship of the nearby tribes was important to aid in his "explorations which, as it seemed, could only be carried out with their help, and also because this would be to them a kind of pathway and preparation for embracing Christianity" (Champlain,1907, 276).

The chiefs promised to raise an army of 2,500 warriors and Champlain agreed to bring as many as he could (Champlain 1907, 277).

Champlain Visits Hurons

On 9 July 1615 Champlain set off from the Saint Louys rapids (Lachine near what is now Montreal) in two canoes with two French and ten Indians. They could carry only the arquebuses, a supply of powder, match, and shot, some trade goods, the barest provision of food (Bishop 215,216).

Heading up the tumultuous Ottawa River, they made long portages around waterfalls and rapids as the river rose 579 feet to Lake Huron. After paddling 700 miles in twenty-two days, they reached the great inland sea of fresh water. Along the way they were greeted, banqueted, and provisioned by old friends (Champlain 1907,278-287).

Champlain noted in his journal that "along the streams there are such a great quantity of blueberries, raspberries and other small fruits. The people here dry these fruits for the winter, as we do plums in France (Champlain 1907,279).

At the mouth of the French River they met a party of three hundred warriors named the Cheveux releves, the High Hairs [later known as the Ottawas], because they wore their hair elevated and arranged very high. Champlain gave their chief a hatchet. "I asked him about his country [Manitoulin Island and north of Georgian Bay], which he drew for me with charcoal on a piece of treebark" (Bishop, 220-221).

As part of his explorations, Champlain visited five of the Huron villages. He estimated 30,000 lived in Huronia, the present county of Simcoe. On 17 August he arrived at the chief village, Cahiague, [near Warminster] for the council of chiefs to plan the great campaign of 1615 (Bishop 222,225).

The Chief, Ochateguin, who had been at Lake Champlain in 1609, was there, as was Darontal, one of the other chiefs of a Huron clan. Champlain assured them "with my fourteen men and their fourteen guns, we can attack the enemy stronghold. We can bring terror into their country, as they have into ours" (Bishop, 226).

The chiefs agreed the time was propitious. They had received word that their brothers the Carantouans [Susquehannas] wished to join them with 500 of their warriors. They lived three days' journey [South Waverly, Pennsylvania] to the south of the Iroquois (Bishop, 226-227).

After the feasts and dances came to an end, 500 warriors assembled. An embassy was sent to the Carantouans to join them at a fixed date for their assault on the Iroquois. It was already 8 September when they set off on roughly the path of the Trent Canal and continued to the eastern part of Lake Ontario hunting and fishing continually. They landed on the New York shore under the high bluff of Stony Point (Bishop, 229-231).

They hid their canoes in the woods near the shore [probably Henderson Bay]. Walking south along the lake shore they came to the mouth of the Salmon River [Selkirk Shores State Park] where Champlain noted:

40

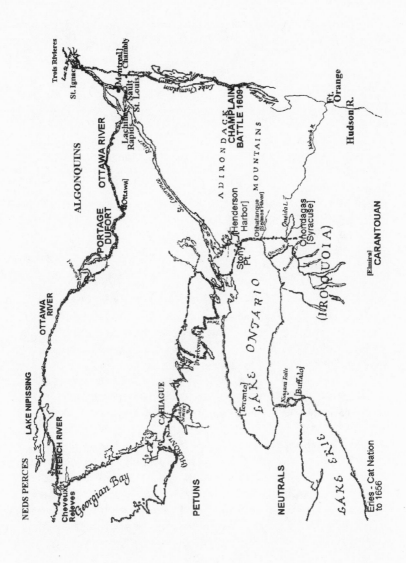

Route of Champlain and his allies to the Iroquois in 1615.

41

Champlain Describes Salmon River Country

We went some four leagues over a sandy strand, where I observed a very pleasant and beautiful country, intersected by many little streams and two small rivers, which discharge into the before-mentioned lake [Ontario] also many ponds and meadows, where there was an endless amount of game, many vines, fine woods, and a large number of chestnut trees, whose fruit was still in the burr. The country is covered with forests, which over its greater portion have not been cleared. (Champlain 1907,289-90).

Turning inland, they headed south along the present route of U.S.Highway No. 11 to the outlet of Oneida Lake at Brewerton, arriving 9 October. The chiefs and Champlain planned to creep up on the enemy fort, ten miles distant, post themselves in the woods for the night, and attack at dawn (Champlain 1907, 291).

Champlain Attacks Iroquois Fort

Arriving at the fort of the enemy [which may have been where Onondaga Creek flows into Onondaga Lake] it was only three in the afternoon. Discovered by some Onondaga warriors, the battle began (Champlain 1907, 290-291; Bradley,224).

Champlain described the scene as follows:

I approached the enemy, and although I had only a few men, yet we showed them what they had never seen nor heard before; for, as soon as they saw us and heard the arquebus shots and the balls whizzing in their ears, they withdrew speedily to their fort, carrying the dead and wounded in this charge. We also withdrew to our main body, with five or six wounded, one of whom died. (Champlain 1907, 291).

The expectation was that the five hundred Carantouans who had promised to come would do so on this day, but they had not appeared. Champlain continued:

42

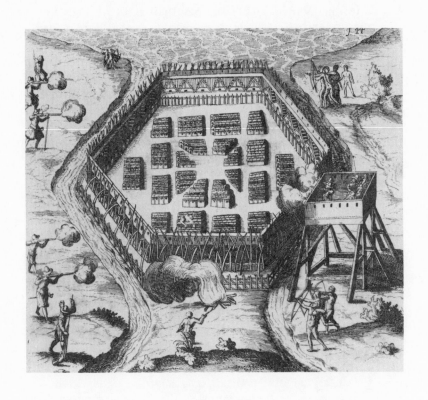

Champlain's drawing of the Iroquois Fort he and his allies attacked in October 1615. From his Voyages and Descouvertures (1619). Courtesy of Library of Congress. Champlain pictures himself at lower left, reloading his arquebus near other French soldiers firing their guns. One is using a tripod for support of the heavy armament. On the right is the cavalier with arquebusiers on top. It is shown with sawn timber, but must have been of logs. Indian attackers are shown on right side with bows and arrows. In the center is a fire set on the wrong side, where wind blows it away from the fort. Streams of water are shown on both sides of the fort flowing into a body of water, probably Onondaga Lake. Longhouses are shown inside the fort around a center square.

43

The enemy had already strengthened themselves very much; for their village was enclosed by four good palisades, which were made of great pieces of wood, interlaced with each other with an opening of not more than half a foot between two, and which were thirty feet high, with galleries after the manner of a parapet, which they had furnished with double pieces of wood that were proof against our arquebus shots. Moreover, it was near a pond where the water was abundant, and was well supplied with gutters, placed between each pair of palisades, to throw out water, which they had also under cover inside in order to extinguish fire (Champlain 1907, 292-93).

With no horses to drag the thirty foot long timbers from the forest to their village, the Iroquois had dragged and raised them and set them in the holes around the village. Champlain continued his account as he showed the attacking Indians how to construct a cavalier, a movable tower overtopping the walls of the fort, from which to fire down on the defenders

We approached to attack the village, our cavalier being carried by 200 of the strongest men, who put it down before the village at a pike's length off. I ordered three-arquebusiers to mount upon it, who were well protected from the arrows and stones that could be shot or hurled at them.

Meanwhile, the enemy did not fail to send a large number of arrows which did not miss, and a great many stones, which they hurled from their palisades. Nevertheless, a hot fire of arquebusiers forced them to disledge and abandon their galleries, in consequence of the cavalier which uncovered them, they not venturing to show themselves, but fighting under shelter. . . .

We were engaged in this combat about three hours, in which two of our chiefs and leading warriors were wounded, namely, one named Ochateguain and another Orani, together with some fifteen common warriors. The others, seeing their men and some of the chiefs wounded, now began to talk of a retreat without farther fighting, in expectation of the five hundred men whose arrival could not be much delayed. Thus they retreated. .. Moreover, the chiefs have in fact no absolute control over their men, who are governed by their own will (Champlain 1907,293-94.

Champlain, as a Frenchman coming from a country ruled by a King, conceived of all power as being delegated from above. He did not understand that the Iroquois leaders were required to secure individual consent from their followers as each new issue arose.

After waiting four days for the other 500 warriors, they gave up hope and decided to retreat. (Their allies came two days later.) Champlain, unable to walk from an arrow wound to his knee and another to his leg, was carried with the other wounded back to Henderson Bay and the hidden canoes. He spent the winter with the Hurons (Bishop,236-42).

In the spring he returned to Quebec with the twelve Frenchmen, Father Joseph and the Interpreter Thomas, and then on to France to obtain further support for New France.

The European firearms could not dislodge the Iroquois from their fortified village without additional forces. The Iroquois remained a formidable enemy.

3

Competition for Beavers

The expansion of Dutch commercial activity along the upper Hudson River created a serious conflict and had a profound effect on the Iroquois Confederacy. "From an Onondaga viewpoint, the Mohawk had all the advantages". They were closest to the Dutch. They could regulate the flow of trade between the Dutch and the other Iroquois nations. "Their geographic location entitled them to certain privileges, of which this was one . . .Jealous protection of this privileged position quickly became the hallmark of Mohawk intertribal relations" (Bradley, 181).

In 1620 the Mohawks stopped the Dutch from expanding their trade directly with the northern Algonquin tribes. By 1628 they had eliminated the Mahicans and strengthened their position (Bradley 181).

In 1634 the Dutch sent one of their men, thought to be Harmen van den Bogaert, and two companions to visit the Oneidas and determine why trade was going very badly. When they reached the Oneida territory, they came to a high point and saw a very large body of water. In answer to their questions about this, the Indians said that the French came into that water to trade for their beaver skins (Jameson 148).

French Trading with Iroquois

In the afternoon one of the council came to me, asking the reason of our coming into his land, and what we brought for him as a present. I told him that we did not bring any present, but that we only paid him a visit. He told us that we were not worth anything because we did not bring him a present. Then he told us how the Frenchmen had come . . . and given them good gifts, because they had been trading in this river with six men in the month of August of this year. We saw very good axes

46

to cut the underwood, and French shirts and coats and razors; and this member of the council said we were scoundrels, and were not worth anything because we paid not enough for their beaver skins.

Gifts were an essential part of Iroquois culture. The practice of reciprocal exchange symbolized friendship, generosity, and hospitality (Richter 47).

In subsequent years the hostilities between the Iroquois and nearby tribes intensified. Overhunting resulted in the disappearance of beavers and other animals from the Iroquois territory. They had to go further distances and raid other tribes for pelts to take to the Dutch (Trelease,118,130).

The Hurons, as trading partners of the French, occupied a territory located north of Lake Ontario and west of Montreal to the Great Lakes. They captured some beavers in this area. In addition, they took French trade goods to far-distant tribes to exchange for a larger supply of pelts to take to the French. Close trading contact with the French also resulted in the rise of Jesuit missions among the Hurons. Many were converted to Christianity (Trigger,351).

Iroquois Raid Hurons

During the 1640's individual Iroquois war-parties raided the Huron and French villages, killing or capturing large numbers of Hurons, as well as some French, and taking their supply of furs.

The Iroquois followed the practice of adopting prisoners to replace the warriors lost, and also to establish a more lasting peace by making their erstwhile enemies a part of their family. Clan mothers played an important role in deciding which captives would be adopted or killed. Those adopted took the place of lost relatives and were treated as true members of the family and of the League. Often whole villages with the captured women and children, became a part of the Iroquois (Trigger,352, 355). Some continued to hold to their Christian beliefs while living among the Iroquois.

In 1648, the scale of the hostilities increased when the Dutch sold the Mohawks 400 guns. It was in their trading interest to increase their supply of furs. During the following year the Senecas and Mohawks destroyed the main Huron villages. Those who were not killed or captured abandoned the country to join other tribes or the French (Trigger,355,356; Jennings 1984,98,99; O'Callaghan 13:23-24).

The Jesuits complained of all this warfare:

"for a year the warehouse of Montreal has not bought a single beaver-skin from the Indians. Before the devastation of the Hurons, a hundred canoes used to come to trade, all laden with beaverskins; and each year we had two or three hundred thousand livres worth. That was a fine revenue with which to satisfy all the people and defray the heavy expenses of the country. The Iroquois war dried up all these springs. The beavers are left in peace and in the place of their repose; the Huron fleets no longer come down to trade; the Algonquins are depopulated; and the more distant nations are withdrawing still farther, fearing the fire of the Iroquois"(Jesuit Relations, hereafter 'J. R.' 40:211).

The French needed a new source of furs.

As for the Iroquois, with no further opposition in the Huron territory, the four Western nations (the Oneidas, the Onondagas, the Cayugas, and the Senecas) began a series of peace negotiations with the French to become their new trading partners. They found the route by water to the French easier; some were annoyed that the Mohawks tried to control access to the Dutch.

The Mohawks, however, benefited greatly when the trade of the western nations had to pass through their country. They tried to block a change. (Jennings 1984,105-106). A serious conflict within the Iroquois Confederacy had arisen.

On 26 June 1653 sixty Onondaga warriors approached Montreal. Calling out from afar, they requested a safe-conduct for some of their number. They said they were sent on "behalf of their whole nation to learn whether the hearts of the French would be inclined to peace" (J.R.40:89).

48

Onondagas Visit Quebec

After all the years of warfare, the French remained armed and fearful as they invited the delegation into their fort. The ambassadors entered without arms "satisfied with the mere word that had been given them for their sole defense." Safe conduct was a custom for them and not expected to be violated (J.R.40:91).

The Governor of Montreal answered that "if they had any desire for an alliance with the French," they must see Monsieur de Lauson, Governor of the whole country, who was at Quebec" (J.R.40:165).

It is significant that political decisions of the Onondagas were made after consultation with "the whole nation" and the message sent through a chosen speaker, while the French Governor alone had the authority to speak for his people.

The Onondaga Ambassador replied that a careful distinction must be made between Nation and Nation . . . that the Onondagas were not faithless. . . As for him "whom the whole Nation had acquainted with its sentiments . . . he would go to see the great Onnontio, Governor of the French, and would offer him his presents, in which were enclosed the wishes of his entire Nation" (J.R.40:165).

The sixty ambassadors split. The Speaker and a few others started to Quebec. The rest carried away to their villages presents from the French - the cloaks, the blankets, kettles, and other commodities - saying they would bring back news of the entire joy of their Nation at the prospect of peace. On the way they called at the Village of the Oneidas reporting on the events at Montreal. As a result, the Oneidas, wishing to be a party to the peace, later sent an embassy to Montreal (J.R.40:91).

The remaining delegates voyaged sixty leagues down the St. Lawrence to the Island of Orleans near Quebec. The first assembly was held in the Village of the Hurons. When everyone was seated, the Onondaga Captain rose, and with typical Iroquoian eloquence "first invoked the sun as a faithful witness of the sincerity of his intentions, and as a torch that banished the night and the darkness from his heart, to let in a veritable daylight upon his word" (J.R.40:165).

49

Porcelain Colliers / Wampum Belts

The Captain displayed his presents of beaverskins and porcelain; and each of them had its name, and testified the desire of the speaker and of those who had delegated him. No agreements were concluded with the Iroquois without the exchange of presents in formal proceedings. What the French called the colliers or porcelain, the English named belts of wampum.

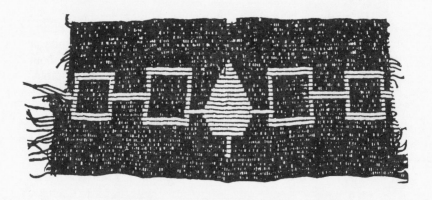

Hiawatha Belt of thirty-eight rows is the symbol of the unity of the Five Nations with the white Tree of Great Peace in the center. It also stands for the Onondagas as the heart of the Confederacy. The Tree is connected to the squares which stand for the Mohawks, Oneidas, Cayugas, and Senecas. White around the squares means peace, love, charity, and equity surround and guard the Five Nations.

The use of strings, wampum belts, or porcelain collars carried "inherent spiritual power in addition to serving as mnemonic devices that recorded transactions. . . . Presents were assurances that promises made in the name of followers were likely to be carried out, for they proved that the speaker had the consent of the kin and followers who had banded together to produce them" (Richter, 47).

Belts and strings of wampum were prepared in advance to accompany each "word" to be presented at a treaty conference. Each family of note provided the beads or shells and, in addition, each village had a "public treasury of valuables that could be drawn on to demonstrate the support of the entire town. Words of peace and gifts of peace, then were inseparable; together, they demonstrated and symbolized the shared climate of good thoughts upon which good relations and powerful alliances depended"(Richter 48).

They had the same use that writings and contracts had with Europeans as records of words spoken and exchanged during transactions. Physically these belts were made of the quahog or round clam shell. They were long, cylinder-shaped beads about one-fourth inch long and one-eighth of an inch in diameter drilled from opposite ends, and "strung in rows with sinew, vegetable fiber and/or thread, forming a rectangular belt that is usually longer than wide. The beads are deep purple (black) or white in color. . . . Belts were made of beads of one color, or, of a combination of black and white beads often strung to form graphic patterns [emblems] of white on black or black on white" (Jennings 1985, 88).

In the design each belt held a message, learned by the speaker and remembered afterwards. Shells were later replaced by beads obtained in trade with the Europeans.

Message of the Onondagas
The Iroquois speaker, taking in hand the first present, offered it:

> to wipe away the tears that are commonly shed upon hearing of the brave warriors killed in battle.
>
> The second was intended to serve as a pleasant draught to counteract whatever of bitterness might remain in the hearts of the French because of the death of their people.

The third was to furnish a piece of bark or a blanket, to put over the dead, for fear the sight of them might renew the old-time dissension.

The fourth was to bury the dead and tread down the earth very hard over their graves, in order that nothing might ever issue from their tombs that could sadden their relatives, and arouse any feeling of revenge in their bosoms.

The fifth was to serve as a wrapping for packing away the implements of war so securely that they would never be touched again in the future.

The sixth, to make clear the river, stained with so much blood. The last, to exhort the Hurons to accept whatever decision Onontio, the great Captain of the French, should choose to make concerning peace (J.R.40:167).

The Governor gave back speech for speech and present for present in requesting an end to making war. The Onondaga delegation left with presents of cloaks, blankets, kettles, etc., saying they would return with further news from their people (J.R. 40:169).

The French considered the speeches of the Onondaga Ambassador over the winter. Finally, they decided to send Father Simon Le Moyne to the Onondagas the next summer to ratify the peace and determine whether a mission could be established there.

Leaving Quebec on 2 July 1654, he proceeded to Montreal, where an assistant and several Indian guides joined him on the journey (J.R.41:91).

A few days later a Mohawk envoy appeared at Quebec to meet the Governor to protest settlement of the French among the Onondagas and request it be among the Mohawks. Describing the League of the Iroquois, he compared it to a longhouse and offered a prediction:

A Mohawk Describes League of the Iroquois

Ought not one to enter a house by the door and not by the chimney or roof of the cabin, unless he be a thief, and wish to take the inmates by surprise? We, the five Iroquois Nations, compose but one cabin; we maintain but one fire; and we have, from time immemorial, dwelt under one and the same roof. [In fact, from the earliest times, these five Iroquois Nations have been called in their own language Hotinnonchiendi, - that is, "the completed cabin," as if to express that they constituted but one family.] Well then, will you not enter the cabin by the door, which is at the ground floor of the house? It is with us Anniehronnons [Mohawks], that you should begin; whereas you, by beginning with the Onnontaehronnons [Onondagas] try to enter by the roof and through the chimney. Have you no fear that the smoke may blind you, our fire not being extinguished, and that you may fall from the top to the bottom, having nothing solid on which to plant your feet? (J.R.41:87,89; Jennings 1984, 105-106)

When the French finally came to establish Sainte Marie, the Onondagas felt they had reasserted their claim as the diplomatic center of the Confederacy. Success for them, however, meant humiliation to the Mohawks. It brought the Mohawk to a "jealousy almost verging on fury . . . the result was intra-Iroquois war" (Bradley 185; J.R.43:129).

This feud was often noted by the Jesuits. It threatened to destroy the League. With the rise of more powerful colonies of European nations, the Iroquois eventually came to realize the importance of arriving at mutual agreement among their five nations in dealing with these external forces.

4

Father le Moyne Journeys to Onondaga

Unaware of the opposition of the Mohawks, Father le Moyne continued on his way to the Onondagas writing a day-by-day account from 17 July to 6 September 1654. In the following excerpts, he comments on the beautiful scenery and the wildlife as he paints a picture of his journey along the waterways of the St. Lawrence River, Lake Ontario, and the Oswego River, as well as, the paths through the forests to Onondaga. It was the route to be followed by those succeeding him in founding Sainte Marie:

17 July: set out from home [Montreal] . . . toward a land unknown to us.

18 July: following constantly the course of the River Saint Lawrence, we encounter nothing but breakers and impetuous floods thickly strewn with rocks and shoals.

19 July: The River continues to increase in width and forms a lake, pleasant to the sight, and eight or ten leagues in length. In the evening a swarm of troublesome mosquitoes gave us warning of rain, which drenched us all night long. It is a pleasure, sweet and innocent beyond conception, to have, under these conditions, no shelter but the trees planted by nature since the creation of the world.

20 July: We see nothing but islands, of the most beautiful appearance in the world, intercepting here and there the course of this very peaceful river. The land toward the North appears to us excellent. Toward the rising sun is a chain of high mountains which we named after Saint Margaret.

21 July: The islands continue. Toward evening we break our bark canoe. It rains all night, and the bare rocks serve us as bed, mattress, and every thing else. He who has God with him, rests calmly anywhere.

54

22 July: The rapids, which for a time are not navigable, compel us to shoulder our little baggage and the canoe that bore us. On the other side of the rapids, I caught sight of a herd of wild cows [deer] proceeding in a very calm and leisurely manner. Sometimes there are seen four or five hundred of them together in these regions.

23 and 24 July: Our pilot having injured himself, we were forced to halt, becoming a prey to the mosquitoes, and to wait patiently - a task often more difficult than facing death itself, because of the annoyances from which, night or day, there is no respite.

Portaging Through the Rapids

25 July: The river is becoming so extremely rapid that we are compelled to leap into the water and drag our canoe after us among the rocks, like a horseman who alights and leads his horse by the bridle. In the evening we arrive at the mouth of lake Saint Ignace, where eels abound in prodigious numbers.

The river flows from west to east, therefore Father Le Moyne was travelling upstream. It remains at sea level and is subject to ocean tides until it reaches Montreal. From there to Lake Ontario, the level rises 246 feet. Today, canals bypass the rapids, and locks lift the ships from one level to another. As part of the St. Lawrence Seaway project opened in 1959, a hydroelectric dam created Lake St. Lawrence and provides electric power to Canada and the United States. Thousands of ships now pass along this route, except during the winter months.

26 July: A high wind accompanied by rain, forces us to land, after proceeding four leagues. A cabin is soon made: bark is stripped from the neighboring trees and thrown over poles planted in the ground on either side, and made to meet in the form of an arbor; and there you have your house complete. Ambition gains no entrance to this palace, and it is every whit as acceptable to us as if its roof were of gold.

27 July: We coast along the shores of the lake, everywhere confronted by towering rocks, now appalling and now pleasing to the eye. It is wonderful how large trees can find root among so many rocks.

Sleeps under canoe in rainstorm

28 July: Nothing but thunder and lightning and a deluge of rain, forcing us to seek the shelter of our canoe, which, turned bottom upward over our heads, serves us as a house.

29 and 30 July: The windstorm continues, and checks our progress at the mouth of a great lake called Ontario; we call it the lake of the Iroquois, because they have their villages on its southern side. The Hurons are on the other side, farther inland. This lake is twenty leagues in width and about forty in length.

31 July: The day of Saint Ignatius we are obliged by the rain and wind to penetrate through pathless wastes, crossing long islands, and shouldering our baggage, our provisions, and the canoe. This road seems long to a poor man who is thoroughly fatigued.

1 August: Some Iroquois fishermen, perceiving us from a distance, come trooping up to receive us. One of them hastens forward, running half a league to be the first to tell us the news, and inform us of the condition of the country. He is a Huron captive and a good Christian, whom I formerly instructed during a winter I spent with the Hurons. This poor lad could not believe that I was his pastor, whom he had never hoped to see again. We land at a little fishing village, and there is zealous strife as to who shall carry all our baggage. . .

2 August: We walk about twelve or fifteen leagues through the woods, and camp where night overtakes us.

3 August: Toward noon we found ourselves on the banks of a river, a hundred or a hundred and twenty paces in width, on the other side of which there was a fishing hamlet. An Iroquois, to whom I had formerly shown some kindness at Montreal, took me across in his canoe;

and then, as a mark of honor, carried me on his
shoulders, not allowing me to set foot in the water.

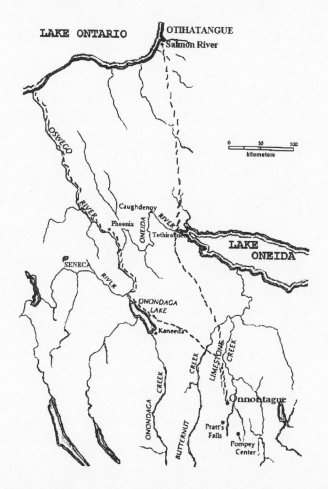

*Route of Rev. Simon le Moyne S.J. to Village of Onondaga,
1654 Taken from "Map of Early Visitors" by William Beauchamp,
Courtesy of Onondaga Historical Association. Also map of "Early
Historic Onondaga Iroquois Sites" by James Bradley, Evolution
of the Onondaga Iroquois, Syracuse University Press, 1987.*

I was escorted to another village, a league distant, where a young man of importance entertained me at a feast, because I bear his Father's name, "Ondessonk." The Captains, each in his turn, came and made us their speeches...

4 August: They ask me why we are dressed in black, and I take occasion to speak to them concerning our mysteries; they listen very attentively. . . . We pursue our journey, finding our dinner awaiting us midway. The nephew of the first Captain of the country is to lodge me in his cabin, being sent by his uncle to escort us, and bringing us all that the season could furnish them in the way of choicest delicacies; above all, some bread made of fresh Indian corn; and some ears, which we roasted in the fire. On this day we again sleep at the sign of the beautiful star.

Arrives at Onontague

5 August: We had four leagues to cover before arriving at the chief village, Onnontage. The roads were full of people going and coming, who are out to greet me. One calls me a brother, another an uncle, another a cousin; never have I had so many kinsfolk. At a quarter of a league from the village, I began a harangue [speech] which brought me into high favor; I called by name all the Captains, families, and persons of importance, speaking slowly and in the tone of a Captain. I told them that Peace was attending my course, that I was dispelling war in the more distant nations, and that joy was accompanying me. Two Captains made me their harangue upon my entrance, but with a joy and a light in their countenances . . . Men, women, and children, all showed me respect and love.

At night I caused the chiefs to assemble, in order to give them two presents. The purpose of the first was to wipe their faces, so that they might look on me with favor, and that I might never see any sign of sadness on their brows. The second was to remove any gall still remaining in their hearts. After several more exchanges of courtesy, they withdrew to consult together; and at length responded to my presents with two others, richer than mine.

August 6: I received calls from different quarters to administer my medicine to some little weak and emaciated children, and I baptized some of them. I heard the confessions of some of our old Huron Christians, and found that God is everywhere, and that he is pleased to work in person in hearts where the faith has held sway. He builds himself a temple there, where he is worshiped in spirit and in truth - for which may he be forever blessed.

In the evening, our host drew me aside and said to me, with a great show of affection, that he had always loved us; and that at last his heart was content, as he saw that all the troops of his nation asked only for Peace. He added that the Sonnontoehronons [Senecas] had come, a short time before, to exhort them to take wise action in this matter on the side of Peace, making some fine presents for this purpose; that the Onioenhronnons [Cayugas] had brought three collars, with the same object in view; that they deemed themselves fortunate to have been freed from a troublesome affair by its means and that they had no longer any desire except for Peace; that the Anniehronnons [Mohawks] would doubtless follow the others; and that, therefore, I was to be of good cheer since I bore with me the welfare of all the land (J.R.41:91-101).

Visits Huron Captives

On the next two days Father Le Moyne visited the Huron Christians (captives who were now part of the Iroquois, living with the Onondagas). He baptized three dying children and spoke about "God, the hopes of eternal life, and the truths of the faith" (J.R.41:103).

59

9 August: Toward noon, there comes a direful report of the murder of three of their hunters at the hands of the Cat Nation [Eries who lived on southern side of what is now Lake Erie], a day's journey from here. That means that war is kindled in that direction.

Delivers Speech

10 August: Envoys from the three neighboring Nations having arrived, after the customary summons of the Captains, to the effect that all should assemble in Ondessonk's cabin. I opened the proceedings with a public prayer, which I offered on my knees and in a loud voice, using the Huron tongue throughout. I appealed to the great master of heaven and earth, that he might inspire us to act for his glory and our own good; I cursed all the Demons of hell, since they are spirits of discord; and I prayed the guardian Angels of the entire country to speak to the hearts of my hearers, when my words should strike their ears.

I astonished them greatly when they heard me name them all by Nations, bands, and families and each person individually who was of some little consequence - all by the help of my written list, which was to them a thing full of both charm and novelty. I told them that in my speech, I had nineteen words [thoughts] to lay before them.

First, I said that Onnontio - Monsieur de Lauson, Governor of New France - was speaking through my mouth, and in his person the Hurons and the Algonquins, as well as the French, since all three Nations had Onnontio for their great Captain. A large Porcelain collar, a hundred little tubes or pipes of red glass [from which wampum is often made and decorations on clothing], which constitute the diamonds of the country, and a moose-skin, somewhat worn, - these three presents accompanied one word only.

60

My second word was to cut the bonds of the eight captives from Sonnontouan [Senecas], who had been taken by our Allies and brought to Montreal . . .

The third was to break also the bonds of those members of the Wolf Nation who had been captured at about the same time.

The fourth, to thank the people of Onontage for bringing back our captive to us.

The fifth present was to thank the people of Sonnontouan for rescuing him from his position on the scaffold [a platform erected for his execution].

The sixth was for the Onioenhronon [Cayugas] Iroquois because they too had helped in this.

The seventh for the Onneiochronnons [Oneidas] in return for breaking the bonds that had held him captive.

The purpose of the eighth, ninth, tenth, and eleventh presents was to give to each of those four Iroquois Nations a hatchet, to be used in the New war in which they were engaged with the Cat Nation.

The twelfth present was intended to renew the courage of the Sonnontoehronnons, who had lost some of their number in this war.

The thirteenth was to strengthen their palisade - that is, to enable them to maintain a strong defense against the enemy.

The fourteenth, to paint their faces, for it is the custom of the warriors here never to go into battle without having their faces painted, - some with black, some with red, and some with various other colors, - each having in this matter his own style of livery, so to speak, which he retains through life.

The fifteenth, to harmonize all their thoughts, for which purpose alone I made three presents, - a porcelain collar, some little glass tubes, and a moose-skin.

With the sixteenth, I opened Annonchiasse's door to all the Nations, - thus indicating that they would be welcome in our cabin.

With the seventeenth, I exhorted them to become instructed in the truths of our faith, making three presents to accompany this word.

With the eighteenth, I asked them to lay no more ambuscades in future for the Algonquin and Huron Nations when they should wish to visit us in our French settlements. I made three gifts with this request.

Finally with the nineteenth present, I wiped away the tears of all the young warriors, caused by the death of their great Captain Anneneraes, who had been taken captive by the Cat Nation not long before.

At each of my presents they uttered a loud shout of applause from the depths of their chests, in evidence of their delight. I was occupied fully two hours in delivering my entire harangue [speech], which I pronounced in the tone of a Captain, - walking back and forth, as is their custom, like an actor on a stage.

After that, they gathered together by Nations and bands, calling to them an Anniehronnon [Mohawk] who by good luck happened to be present. They consulted together for more than two hours longer, when they at length called me back and gave me a seat of honor among them (J.R.41:107-115).

The Onondagas Reply

Then one of the Captains who is the tongue of the Country and acts as its orator, repeated faithfully the substance of all that I had said. Then they all began to sing to express their joy; and told me that I might, for my part, pray to God, which I did very willingly.

After these songs, he addressed me in the name of his nation:

"1. He thanked Onnontio for the good will he entertained toward them, in token whereof he produced two large Porcelain collars.

"2. In the name of the Anniehronnon [Mohawk] Iroquois, he thanked us for causing the lives of five of

62

their allies, of the Wolf Nation, to be spared, -therewith, two more collars.

"3. In the name of the Sonnontoehronnon [Seneca] Iroquois, he thanked us for rescuing from the flames five of their people, and this with two more collars. Each present was followed by applause from the whole assembly.

Another Captain, of the Nation of the Onneiocronnons [Oneidas] arose. "Onnontio," said he, addressing Monsieur de Lauson, our absent Governor, "Onnontio, thou art the support of the earth; thy spirit is a spirit of Peace, and thy words soften the most rebellious hearts." After other praises, which he uttered in a tone animated with affection and respect, he displayed four large collars, with which to thank Onnontio for encouraging them to make a spirited fight against their new enemies of the Cat Nation, and for exhorting them never to wage war again with the French. "Thy voice, Onnontio," said he, "is wonderful, for it produces in my heart, at the same time, two wholly opposite emotions. Thou givest me courage to fight, and thou softenest my heart with thoughts of Peace. Thou art both peaceable and yet very warlike, - beneficent to those thou lovest, and terrible to thy enemies. We all wish thee to love us, and we shall love the French for thy sake" (J.R.41:115,117).

To conclude these thanksgivings, the Onnontaer-honnon Captain took the word: "Listen Ondessonk," he said to me; "Five whole Nations address thee through my mouth; I have in my heart the sentiments of all the Iroquois Nations and my tongue is faithful to my heart.

Onondagas Invite French to Lake Gannentaha
Thou shall tell Onontio four things, which are the gist of all our deliberations in Council:"
"1. It is our wish to acknowledge him of whom thou hast told us, who is the master of our lives, and who is un-known to us.

"2. "The May-tree for all matters of concern to us is to-day planted at Onnontage." He meant that would be thenceforth the scene of the assemblies and parleys relating to the peace.

"3. We conjure you to choose a site that will be advantageous to yourselves, on the shores of our great lake, in order to build thereon a French settlement. Place yourselves in the heart of the country, since you are to possess our hearts. Thither we will go to receive instruction, and thence you will be able to spread out in all directions. Show us paternal care and we will render you filial obedience.

"4. We are involved in new wars, wherein Onontio gives us courage; but for him we shall have only thoughts of peace" (J.R.41:117).

They had reserved their richest presents to accompany these last four words; but I am sure that their countenances spoke more eloquently than their tongues, and joy was depicted on their faces, with so much kindness that my heart was deeply moved . . .

11 August: There was nothing but feasting and rejoicing on every hand. At night, however, a disaster befell us: a cabin having caught fire, - we know not how, - a furious wind carried the flames to the others; and in less than two hours more than twenty of them were reduced to ashes, while the rest of the village was in danger of destruction. Nevertheless, God maintained the spirits of all in the joy of the preceding day, and kept their hearts as calm toward me as if this misfortune had not occurred.

13 August: In regard to the conflagration that had occurred, in order to follow the custom of friends on such occasion, I convoked the council and gave the people two presents to console them.

Accordingly, in the name of Achiendasse [the superior general of all the Missions of our Society in these regions] I began by planting for them the first stake for a new cabin; this corresponds to our French custom of laying the foundation-stone of a new building.

64

The purpose of my second present was to throw down the first piece of bark that was to cover the cabin. This mark of affection gratified them and three of their captains thanked me for it publicly in speeches. . .

14 August: A young Captain, chief of a levy of eighteen hundred men who were to set out as soon as possible to prosecute the war against the Cat Nation, begged me urgently for baptism. For several days I had been giving him instruction, and, as I wished to make him prize this mark of grace by deferring it until some future journey, he said to me: "How now, my brother? If from this day forth I possess the Faith, cannot I be a Christian? Hast thou power over death to forbid its attacking me without orders from thee? Will our enemies' arrows become blunted for my sake? Dost thou wish me at each step that I take in battle, to fear hell more than death? Unless thou baptize me, I shall be without courage, and shall not dare to face the conflict. Baptize me, for I am determined to obey thee; and I give thee my word that I will live and die a Christian" (J.R.41:123).

15 August: Early in the morning, I lead my Catechumen aside, and, seeing his heart piously inclined toward baptism, give him the name of my dear traveling companion, Jean Baptiste. He embraces me, pours out his heart to me in love and solemnly declares that Jesus shall be his only hope and his all.

Meanwhile, the others seek for me everywhere, that I may give the Farewell feast; all the people of importance, both men and women, are invited into our cabin, in my name, according to the custom of the country, to honor my departure.

Leaves for Quebec

We take our leave well attended, after public proclamations of the Captains as to who shall carry our little baggage. Half a league from there, we meet a number of elders, all members of the council, who are waiting for me in order to bid me farewell, in the hope that I shall

65

return; and they evince an ardent desire to see this hope fulfilled.

Discovers Salt Wells

16 August: We arrive at the entrance to a little lake in a great basin that is half dried up [Onondaga Lake], and taste the water from a spring which these people dare not drink, as they say there is an evil spirit in it that renders it foul. Upon tasting it, I find it to be a spring of salt water; and indeed we made some salt from it, as natural as that which comes from the sea, and are carrying a sample of it to Quebec. [Salt was used to preserve foods at the time of no refrigeration.] This lake is very rich in salmon-trout and other fish.

17 August: We enter their river and, a quarter of a league from there, on the left we come to that of the Sonnontouan [Senecas] which swelles the current of the former and leads, they say, to Onioen [Cayugas] and Sonnontouan in two days' journey. Proceeding three leagues from that point, by a very easy route, we leave on the right hand the River Oneiout [Oneida], which appears very deep to us. Finally, a good league farther down, we come to a shoal which gives its name to a fishing village

18 August: My boatmen were repairing their canoes. . .

19 August: We push forward down the same river, which is of a fine width and deep throughout, with the exception of some shoals where we must step into the water and drag the canoe after us, lest the rocks break it.

Paddling with the swift current downstream was easier. The Oswego River, at the junction of the Seneca and Oneida Rivers, is 363 feet above sea level, and descends 118 feet to Lake Ontario during the course of 23.4 miles. Seven locks enable river traffic to bypass the rapids and waterfalls now.

20 August: We arrived at the great lake Ontario, called the Lake of the Iroquois.

66

21 August: This lake is in violent commotion owing to the furious winds that followed a rainstorm.

22 August: Crossing quietly along the shores of this great lake, my boatmen shoot at and kill a large stag. My companion and I content ourselves with looking at them while they broil their steaks, it being Saturday, a day of abstinence for us.

23 August: We arrive at the spot which is to become our dwelling place and the site of a French settlement [perhaps Sackett's Harbor]. There are beautiful prairies here and good fishing; it is a resort for all Nations. I find some new Christians who confess and inspire me with devotion by their sentiments of piety.

24 and 25 August: We were detained by the wind

26 August:: Our boatmen having embarked before the storm had subsided, one of our canoes sprang a leak, and we narrowly escaped drowning; but at last we took refuge on an island, where we dried ourselves at our leisure.

27 August: Toward evening a slight calm gives us time to regain the mainland.

Boatmen Go Hunting

28 and 29 August: Hunting detains my boatmen, who are in the best humor in the world; for flesh is the Paradise of a man of flesh.

30 and 31 August: The rain and wind greatly annoy poor travelers who, after toiling during the day, are badly used all night.

1 September: I never saw so many deer; but we had no desire to hunt them, though my companion killed three almost in spite of himself. What a pity! for we left all the venison there, except some of the more delicate portions, and the skins.

2 September: While proceeding across vast prairies, we see in different places large herds of wild cattle; their horns resemble in many respects the antlers of a stag.

<u>3 and 4 September:</u> Our success in the chase does not abate, game and venison appearing to follow us everywhere. Herds of twenty cows leap into the water . . . and our men, for sheer sport, kill some of them with their hatchets.

<u>5 September:</u> We cover in one day the same distance that we scarcely accomplished in two long days' journey on our way up, through rapids and breakers.

<u>6 September:</u> Our sault St. Louis frightens my men. They put me ashore four leagues above the settlement of Montreal, and God gives me strength enough to reach that place before noon and to celebrate Holy Mass, of which I have been deprived during my entire journey.

<u>7 September:</u> I pass on, and go down toward Three Rivers, whither my boatmen wish to go. We arrived at Quebec only on the eleventh day of the month of September of this year 1654 (J. R. 41:107-129)

5

The Onondagas Invite the French

After the visit of Father le Moyne to the Onondagas, many councils were held by the Iroquois during the following winter. All the sachems of the League had to be of "one mind" to act on proposals. Unanimity was a fundamental law. When, however, all efforts to produce agreement failed, the whole matter was laid aside (Morgan 111, 113).

The Peacemaker illustrated the importance of agreement by all when he took a bundle of arrows and said:

> We have now completed this union by securing one arrow from each nation. It is not good that one should be lacking or taken from the bundle, for it would weaken our power and it would be still worse if two arrows were taken from the bundle. And if three arrows were taken, anyone could break the remaining arrows in the bundle.
>
> We shall tie this bundle of arrows together with deer sinew which is strong, durable and lasting, and then also this institution shall be strong and unchangeable. This bundle of arrows signifies that all the lords and all the warriors and all the women of the Confederacy become united as one person.
>
> We have now completed binding this bundle of arrows and we shall leave it beside the great tree and beside the Confederate Council fire of Thadodahho (Fenton 101, 102).

Evidently there was not a unanimous decision on seeking peace with the French. In this case, the Oneida, Onondaga, Cayuga and Seneca decided to send an embassy. The upper Iroquois wished to confirm the peace, not only with the French, but also the Algonquins and Hurons. However, the Mohawks

69

were not included, as it would destroy their position as the channel of trade between the Iroquois and the Dutch.

Onondagas Send Delegation to Quebec

In the summer of 1655, eighteen Onondagas returned to Quebec to see Monsieur de Lauson, Governor of the country (J.R.42:49). On Sunday, 12 September 1655, at noon a great crowd assembled. The Chief Ambassador, in the Iroquois ritual ceremony of diplomacy, spread out twenty-four collars of porcelain [wampum] to express separately the matters to be considered. The first eight were to make peace with the Algonquins and Hurons.

> You have wept too much, . . . it is time to wipe away the tears shed so plentifully by you over the death of those whom you have lost in war. Here is a handkerchief for that purpose (J.R. 42:51).
>
> The purpose of the second was to wipe away the blood which had crimsoned mountains, lakes, and rivers, and which was crying for vengeance against those who had shed it.
>
> Exhibiting the third present he said "I wrest from your hands hatchet, bows, and arrows, and to strike the evil at its root, I take away all thoughts of war from your hearts" (J.R 42:51).
>
> These people believe that sadness, anger, and all violent passions expel the rational soul from the body, which, meanwhile, is animated only by the sensitive soul which we have in common with animals. That is why, on such occasions, they usually make a present to restore the rational soul to the seat of reason. Such was the fourth present.
>
> The fifth was a medicinal draught to expel from their hearts all the bitterness, gall, and bile with which they might still be irritated.
>
> The sixth present was to open their ears to the words of truth and the promises of a genuine peace in the

70

knowledge that passion stupefies and blinds those who yield to it.

The seventh, to give assurance that the four upper Iroquois Nations were peacefully inclined, and that their hearts would never be divided. "There remains only the lower Iroquois, the Agnieronnon [Mohawk], who cannot restrain his warlike spirit. His mind is ever inflamed, and his hands delight in blood. We will take the war-hatchet out of his hands, and check his fury; for the reign of Peace must be universal in this country" (J.R.42:53). That was the eighth present. . . .

The following were for the French, being addressed to Monsieur our Governor, whom they call Onnontio; one, to dry the tears of the French; another, to wash away the blood that had been shed; another, to soothe our feelings; and the last, to serve us as a medicine, and as a draught sweeter than sugar and honey.

The thirteenth present was an invitation to Monsieur, our Governor, to send a company of Frenchmen to their country, in order to make but one people of us, and to confirm an alliance like that formerly contracted by us with the Huron Nation during our residence there.

The fourteenth was a request for some Fathers of our Society, to teach their children and make of them a thoroughly Christian people.

They further asked for French soldiers, to defend their villages against the inroads of the Cat Nation with whom they are at open war. That was their fifteenth present.

Request to Build New Sainte Marie

The object of the sixteenth present was to assign us a place in the center of all their Nations, where we hope, if God favors our undertakings, to build a new Sainte Marie, like that whose prosperity we formerly witnessed in the heart of the Huron country.

But, that the annoyances commonly attending the founding of a new settlement might not deter us, they spread out a mat and some campbeds for our greater comfort and repose.

The eighteenth present was a May-tree, which they erected in front of that new house of Sainte Marie, so high that it reached the clouds. By this they meant that the center of the Peace, and the place for general reunions, would be in that house, before which should be erected this great May-tree, so lofty that it could be seen from every direction, and all the Nations, even those most distant, could come to it.

The purpose of the nineteenth present was to fix the Sun high in the Heavens above this May-tree -- so as to shine directly down upon it, and admit of no shadow, - in order that all councils held and treaties concluded there might take place, not in the obscurity of night, but in open day, lighted by the Sun, which sees all things and has only abhorrence for treasonable plots, which court darkness.

They next lighted a fire for all who should visit us in that place.

The twenty-first present strengthened Onnontio's arms, [They asked that the relationship of the Hurons and the French be extended to the Iroquois.] "Thou Onnontio hast sustained life in all the nations that became thy allies and took refuge in thy arms. Clasp them more firmly, and weary not of embracing them, let them live within thy bosom, for thou art the Father of the country" (J.R.42:55).

The twenty-second present assured us that the four upper Iroquois Nations had but one heart and one mind in their sincere desire for peace. After that they asked for weapons against the Cat Nation.

Finally, the last of the presents was offered by a Huron Captain, formerly a captive of the Iroquois, and now a Captain among them. This man, rising after the Chief of the Embassy had finished, addressed the Hurons as follows: "My Brothers I have not changed my soul despite my change of country, nor has my blood become Iroquois, although I dwell among them. My heart is all

72

Huron, as well as my tongue. I would keep silence were there any deceit in these negotiations for peace. Our proposals are honest; embrace them without distrust" (J.R.42:57).

French Send Two Jesuits

The French noticed a breakdown in the unity among the members of the League - that the Mohawks were not part of the embassy. Questioning whether there was a trap to kill them, they were greatly divided about accepting this invitation.

Finally, they agreed to send Father Joseph Chaumonot, who knew the language and was friendly with the Indians, and Father Claude d'Ablon, who had recently arrived from France with heart and soul bent upon going to a mission (J.R. 42:57). The Jesuit writer continued:

> Monsieur the Governor was of the opinion that we must risk all for the sake of winning all, as it was to be feared that, if we allowed this opportunity to pass by, our course would cause a rupture of the Peace, as showing too evident distrust on our part. His council agreed with him; the Fathers likewise, upon whom this blessed lot had fallen, doubted not that it was their duty to depart upon this Mission, since they were under-taking it for the glory of God and for the salvation of souls whose Angels were calling us to their aid, and in whose behalf the charity of Jesus Christ must solicit our help. Finally on the nineteenth of September, our Fathers and these Ambassadors left us (J.R.42:59).

Excerpts from Father d'Ablon's journal reveal their experiences. As could be expected, the passage through the Saint Louys rapids (Lachine) was rough and difficult. A few days later, when their provisions were short, their hunters killed eight bears which they butchered and cooked. Two days later they killed thirty bears. "One of the ceremonies of the feast that followed this great slaughter was the drinking of bear's fat after the meal, as one drinks hippocras [wine] in France. Then they rubbed

73

themselves from head to foot with that oil, for in truth, bear's fat when melted, resembles oil" (J.R. 42:65).

Onondagas Take a Sweat

A few days later one of the Indians awoke during the night, all out of breath, trembling, crying out, and tossing about like a maniac. While racing about he leaped into the river and had to be dragged out. A fire was made for him, as he said he was very cold. A potion was prepared, but he refused to drink it.

He said that he dreamed that a certain animal, whose nature it is to plunge into the water, had awakened him and jumped into his stomach; that in order to fight the creature he had leaped into the river; and that he was determined to vanquish it. Then all fear turned to laughter.

Still, it was necessary to cure the man's diseased imagination; they all, therefore pretended to be mad like him, and to have to fight animals which plunge into the water [group therapy?]. Thereupon, they prepared to take a sweat, to induce him to do so with them.

[In a small hut or tent, water is run over large, red-hot stones similar to a sauna today. Several persons sitting close together work themselves into excessive perspiration, while singing and talking; and on issuing thence, even at the beginning of winter, they plunge into some half-frozen lake or river, from which, inexplicable though it seem, they return without distress. They do this from superstition, for cleanliness, for health, and for pleasure; it is thus that they refresh and invigorate themselves in the midst of long journeys, and obviate fatigue upon returning (J.R.38:253,255)].

While he was crying and singing at the top of his voice in the little tent used as a sweat-box, and imitating the cry of the animal with which he was contending, they too began, every man of them, to cry and sing . . . a score of voices imitating ducks, teals, frog . . . what a spectacle,

74

to see people counterfeiting madness in order to cure a madman.

Finally they succeeded; for after our man had perspired well and become thoroughly tired, he lay down on his mat and slept peacefully as if nothing had happened. His ailment, coming in a dream, disappeared like a dream in his sleep . . . .

Early on the 24th, we reached Lake Ontario, at the entrance to which five stags were killed toward evening. Nothing further was needed to arrest our company's progress. We contemplated at leisure the beauty of this lake, which is midway between Montreal and Onontague. It marks, however, the end of by far the more difficult half. Furious rapids must be passed, which serve as the outlet of the Lake; then one enters a beautiful sheet of water, sown with various islands distant hardly a quarter of a league from each other. It is pleasant to see the herds of cows or deer swimming from isle to isle (J.R. 42:65,67,69).

On the 25th, we advanced 8 leagues up the Lake's mouth, which is barely three-quarters of a league wide. . .

View of Lake Ontario

We entered the Lake itself on the 26th, proceeding seven or eight leagues. Such a scene of awe-inspiring beauty I have never beheld, - nothing but islands and huge masses of rock, as large as cities, all covered with cedars and firs. The Lake itself is lined with high crags, fearful to behold, for the most part overgrown with cedars. Toward evening, we crossed from the North to the South side.

On the 27th, we proceeded 12 good leagues through a multitude of Islands, large and small, after which we saw nothing but water on all sides. In the evening, we met a party of Sonontouaronon [Seneca] hunters, who were eager to see us; and, in order to do so more at their ease, they invited us to a feast of Indian corn and beans, cooked in clear water, without seasoning. This dish has its charms, when flavored with a bit of genuine love.

Describes Salmon River

Toward 9 o'clock on the morning of the 29th, we arrived at Otihatangue [Salmon River] where we were offered the kettle of welcome, and all crowded about to see us eat.

Otihatangue is a river emptying into Lake Ontario, narrow at its mouth, but very wide, as a rule for the rest of its course. It flows through meadows, which it fertilizes and cuts up into many islands, high and low, all suitable for raising grain.

Such is the richness of this stream that it yields at all seasons various kinds of fish. In the spring, as soon as the snows melt, it is full of gold-colored fish; next come carp, and finally the achigen [black bass]. The latter is a flat fish, half a foot long, and of very fine flavor.

Then comes the brill; and at the end of May, when strawberries are ripe, sturgeon are killed with hatchets. All the rest of the year until winter, the salmon furnishes food to the Village of the Onontae [Onondaga].

We made our bed last night on the shore of the lake [Oneida] where the Iroquois, toward the end of winter, break the ice and catch fish, - or, rather, draw them up by the bucketful. This was our first lodging in the country of the Onontaeronnons [Onondagas], who received us with profuse demonstrations of friendship. A score of Hurons, who were here fishing, showed their joy at seeing Father Chaumonot (J.R.42:71,73). . . .

On the 30th, we left the water and prepared for our trip overland to Onontague. In the afternoon, there appeared 60 Oneoutchoueronon [Oneida] warriors, on their way to fight the so-called Neds Perces, beyond the rapids. [The Beaver tribe of Algonquin located on the north shore of what is now Georgian Bay.] They were led by Atondatochan, the same who came to Montreal in the second embassy sent by the village of Oneout

76

[Oneida]. He is a man of fine appearance, and an eloquent speaker. He begged us to stay here one day longer, that he might learn our errand. (J.R.42:75,77).

These warriors having all assembled on the 31st, Father Chaumonot, after the ceremonies customary on such occasions, addressed Atondatochan; he said, first that he congratulated himself and thanked God at seeing that great man, whose voice had rung out so loud at Montreal that it was still to be heard there, so great was its strength.

In the second place he said that he was led to visit that country in order to secure the fulfillment of his promise, to speak from that time but the same language, to have but one Sun and one heart,- in short, to be thenceforth brothers.

These two clauses were received with the customary applause, and the faces of all showed how much they enjoyed this speech.

In the third place, as the report had spread hither that peace had been concluded between the French and the Annieronons [Mohawks] without including the Algonquins and Hurons, the Father added that he had come to negotiate a genuine peace between all parties.

And, in the fourth place, he presented 1500 porcelain beads, in order to solicit kind treatment for the two Frenchmen who were among those whom they were going to fight. He also prayed the maker of all things to watch over Atondatochan's expedition (J.R.42:77). . . .

After the Father had spoken for half an hour, the Chief began the song of response; and all commenced to sing, in wondrous harmony, in a manner somewhat resembling our plain-chant. [Hymns half-sung and half-spoken.] The first song said that it would take all the rest of the day to thank the Father for so good a speech as he had made them.

The second was to congratulate him upon his journey and his arrival. They sang a third time to light him a fire, that he might take possession of it. The fourth song made us all relatives and brothers; the fifth hurled the hatchet into the deepest abyss, in order that peace might reign in all these countries; and the sixth was designed to make the French masters of the river Otihatangue.

At this point the Chief invited the salmon, brill, and other fish, to leap into our nets, and to fill that river for our service only. He told them they should consider themselves fortunate to end their lives so honorably; named all the fishes of that river, down to the smallest, making a humorous address to each kind; and added a thousand things besides, which excited laughter in all those present.

The seventh song pleased us still more, its purpose being to open their hearts, and let us read their joy at our coming. At the close of their songs, they made us a present of 2,000 porcelain beads.

Then the Father raised his voice and told the Chief that his fine powers of speech would ever increase in volume; that, hitherto, they had resounded through all the confines of Lake Ontario, but, in future, they would speed across the greatest of all Lakes, and be heard as thunder throughout France. At this the Chief and all his followers were extremely pleased. They then invited us to the feast which concluded the ceremonies. (J.R.42:79-81).

We started overland for Onontague on the 1st of November. . . . At the end of five good leagues, we passed the night by the side of a brook, and broke camp at dawn on the 2nd of November. After making 6 or 7 leagues, we lodged at our invariable hostelry, namely, the beautiful Star, leaving it on the 3rd before sunrise . . . to follow our guides, who were leading us that day to Tethiroguen, [Oneida River]. (J.R.42:81).

As soon as we had reached this stream, the more notable men among a large number, whom we found fishing there, came to salute us, and then led us to the most comfortable cabins.

On the 4th of November, we covered about six leagues, still on foot and encumbered with our small baggage. We passed the night in a field, 4 leagues from Onontague. (J.R.42:83).

Welcome to Onontage

On the 5th of November, 1655, as we were continuing our journey, a Captain of note, named Gonaterezon, came a good league to meet us. He made us halt, pleasantly congratulated us upon our arrival, put himself at the head of our Company, and gravely led us to a spot a quarter of a league from Onontague, where the Elders of the country awaited us.

When we had seated ourselves beside them, they offered us the best dishes they had, especially some squashes cooked in the embers. While we were eating, one of the elders, a captain named Okonchiarennen, arose, imposed silence, and harangued us a good quarter of an hour.

He said, among other things, that we were very welcome, our coming had been earnestly desired and long awaited; and since the young men, who breathed only war, had themselves asked for and procured peace, it was for them, the elders, to lay aside their arms and to ratify and embrace it in all sincerity, as they did.

He added that only the Mohawks were bent on darkening the sun, which we made so bright by our approach; and he alone generated clouds in the air, at the very time when we dissipated them; but all the efforts of that envious one would fail, and they would finally have us in their midst. Courage, then; we were to take possession of our domains, and enter our new home with all assurance (J.R.42:85). . . .

Father [Chaumonot] made answer that his speech was a very agreeable draught to us, and took away all the fatigue of our journey; that he came on Onnontio's behalf to satisfy their demands; and that he doubted not that they would be content when they learned his errand. All the people listened with attention and admiration,

79

delighted to hear a Frenchman speak their language so well.

Then he, who had introduced us, arose, gave the signal, and led us through a great crowd of people, - some of whom were drawn up in rows to see us pass through their midst, while others ran after us, and still others offered us fruit, until we came to the village, the streets of which were carefully cleaned and the cabin-roofs crowded with children. At length, a large cabin which had been prepared for us, received us and also all the people it could hold (J.R.42:87).

All the rest of the day and the next they were invited to feasts of bear, beaver and fish at different cabins and exchange of presents.

Onondaga's Proposals

On the 7th, Sunday a secret council of 15 Chiefs was held with Father Chaumonot. In this assembly they made four proposals to the Father:

1. That Agochiendaguete - who is, as it were, the King of this country - and Onnontio had voices of equal power and firmness, and that nothing could sever so suitable a tie which held them in such close union. [The emphasis on power shared, as in the Iroquois League -- not power imposed by one on all, as in the French experience.]
2. They would give some of their most active young men to conduct home the Huron ambassadors who had come with us to treat of Peace.
3. They begged that Onnontio might be informed that if some one of their own people should be ill-treated or even killed by Mohawks, yet that would not hinder the alliance, and they desired the same assurance on Onnontio's part in case an ill befell the French from the same quarter.
4. In the fourth place, as they had learned that the most acceptable thing they could do, in Onontio's eyes, would

be to inform him that autumn that they had erected a Chapel for the Believers, they said that, to please him, they would take steps to that end at the earliest moment (J.R.42:89,91).

A few days later on 11 November, they visited the salt spring, four leagues distant and near the lake called Gannentaha [Onondaga]. Father d'Ablon wrote the following description:

Select Site for Sainte Marie

This is the site chosen for the French settlement on account of its central position among the four Iroquois Nations, - being accessible to them by canoe, over rivers and lakes which make communication free and very easy.

Hunting and fishing render this position an important one, for besides the fish caught there at different seasons, eels are so abundant in the summer that a man can harpoon as many as a thousand in one night; and, as for game, which is always abundant in the winter, turtle-doves [passenger pigeons] from all the country round flock thither toward spring in so great numbers that they are caught in nets.

The spring, from which very good salt is made, issues within a beautiful prairie, surrounded by full-grown forests. At a distance of 80 or 100 paces from this salt spring is found another of fresh water; and these two, though of opposite characters, have their sources in the bosom of the same hill (J.R.42:95,97).

On Monday, November 15th, between nine and ten o'clock in the morning, - after a little dying infant had been secretly sent to Paradise by the waters of Baptism, - all the elders and the people assembled in a public place, in compliance with our request, as we wished to satisfy the general curiosity.

We began with public prayers. Then the Father [Chaumonot] adopted the people of Oiogoen as his children. After this, he displayed a large porcelain collar [wampum], saying that his mouth was Onnontio's, and the words he was about to utter were the words of the French, Hurons and Algonquins, who all spoke through him.

Speech of Father Chaumonot

The first present was intended to hush the cries heard everywhere by the Father, and to wipe away the tears that he saw coursing down their cheeks. But, since it did not suffice to wipe them away, and as he could not dry up this stream while the source was still running, he offered a second present to calm their minds, the seat of all these griefs; and, as the seat of the mind is in the head, he made them a crown of the proffered collar, which he put on the head of each one successively.

At first they were surprised at this novelty; they were pleased, however, when they saw the Father holding a little kettle, full of an excellent beverage, of which he made them all drink, as a third present - in order to dispel their grief and apply the remedy to their very heart and bowels. This was accompanied by a beautiful collar. And in order to wipe away the blood, and implant joy in every breast, leaving no trace of sadness anywhere, the Father presented four Beaver-skins to the four Iroquois Nations, one for each.

The 9th present affected them even more. He brought forward a small tree, whose upper branches bore the names of their deceased captains, and were lopped off to signify their death; but the tree had many other branches, strong and in full leaf, representing their children, through whom these departed Heroes would be restored to life in the persons of their descendants. This tree attracted much more attention that the beads accompanying it.

The two following gifts were to assure them that Annenrai and Tehaionhacoua, two famous Captains killed in war,- the former of whom had taken an oath of fidelity before the Governor of Montreal, and the latter had died invoking Heaven,- to give assurance, I say, that these two brave men were not dead but continued as firmly united with the French as the collars, presented in their name, were inseparably attached to each other.

The 11th present pleased them still more; for the Father, drawing out his handkerchief, showed them therein, on the one side the ashes of a certain Teotegouisen, buried at Three Rivers, and on the other those of the French; and mixing them together, he declared that the Iroquois and the French were but one, both before and after death. He added a second collar to the one accompanying these ashes, to restore that man to life (J.R. 42:101,103,105). . . .

The most beautiful collar of all was produced by the Father, when he said that all he had thus far offered was but a lenitive [softening] and slight alleviation for their woes; he could not prevent them from being ill, or from dying, but he had a very sovereign remedy for all sorts of afflictions. That was properly what brought him to their country, and they had given excellent proof of their good sense in going down to Kebec [Quebec] in quest of him. This great remedy was the Faith, which he came to proclaim to them and which they would doubtless receive with a favor equal to their wisdom in asking for it. The Father then preached in what was really the Italian style, having a sufficient space for walking about and for proclaiming with pomp, the word of God (J.R.42:105). . . .

The addition of another present was necessary, to exonerate the Faith from the calumnies circulated against it by the devil's agents. In order to impress his meaning upon their minds, he showed them a fair sheet of white paper, symbolizing the integrity, innocence and purity of the Faith; and another, all soiled and blackened, whereon were written the calumnies uttered against it. The latter sheet was torn and burnt according as these lies were answered and refuted (J.R.42:105,107). . . .

As a relief to all this, there followed the present of the Ursuline Mothers of Kebec [Quebec], who made a cordial offer to receive into their house the little girls of the country for education. . . . Then came the present of the Hospital Mothers, who had quite recently built a large and splendid Hospital, for the careful reception and charitable nursing of any sick persons of the Nation who might be at Kebec.

With the 17th present we asked that a Chapel be erected as soon as possible . . . and with the Eighteenth that the supplies be provided necessary for us during our Winter's labors among them.

The four following were a pledge that in the following spring some young Frenchmen would come, and they must then launch their canoes early and go to receive them; and that these, upon their arrival, would erect a palisade for the public defense. They were also advised to prepare at the same time the Mat for receiving the Algonquins and Hurons who would follow the French (J.R. 42:107).

The next two presents were an invitation to the two other Nations to move their villages nearer, in order the better to share the advantage of the vicinity of the French (J.R. 42:107). . . .

With the present next to the last, the Father cleared his path for walking, with head erect, through all the Iroquois villages, and gave them like liberty to traverse the entire country of the French (J.R.42:107).

On the seventeenth we were taken out to make measurements for a chapel. It was erected the following day (J.R.42:125).

During the winter the priests conducted ceremonies, taught Christian doctrine, baptized many who were dying and conducted prayer services. Some accepted the Jesuits with joy, but others opposed them.   On 29 February, at a council, the elders said:

Request for Mission
they had been awaiting the coming of the French for more than three years, but had always been put off from year to year, until at last they were tired of so many

postponements; and if the affair were not settled now, it was needless to think any more about it, for they would break with us entirely, in view of the continued delay. They added further that they knew well that it was not trade which brought us to their country, but solely the Faith, which we wished to make known to them.

"Why do you not come at once," they asked, "since you see our whole village embracing it? All this winter the chapel has been crowded, for prayers and instruction; you have been very well received in all the cabins, when you visited them to teach the inmates; and you cannot doubt our wishes after receiving so solemn a present from us, with such public protestations that we are believers" (J.R.42:201).

Fearing to lose so favorable an opportunity, we sought every possible way to send word to Quebec of their state of mind, and to hasten the coming of the French. But no one would undertake to conduct one of us to Quebec, fearing to let slip the season for securing beavers and a whole year's supplies; (J.R.42:203).

Finally, two young warriors and several others agreed to escort Father d'Ablon. The leader was a young convert "named Jean Baptiste who was the first of the Iroquois baptized in perfect health" (J.R. 42:205). On 2 March 1656 the expedition left Onondaga for Quebec. Father d'Ablon described in detail each day of the four-week journey during the cold spring weather, but it can be summarized by one of the days:

we passed all the seventeenth with feet in the water, weather rough and road frightful. At times we had to climb with feet and hands over mountains of snow; again to walk over great ice-blocks, to pass over marshes, plunge into thickets, fell trees for bridging rivers, cross streams and avoid precipices; while, at day's end, we had made barely four short leagues. Finally, to comfort us, we lodged at an inn where there was neither bread nor wine nor bed; but truly God was wholly there (J.R.42:211).

6

The Expedition Travels to Onondaga

Arriving in Montreal on 30 March 1656, Father d'Ablon presented the case for establishing a mission at the Onondagas, as they had demanded. He and Father Chaumonot had spent the winter in their village. They were welcomed and encouraged to establish a settlement.

However, not everyone was in favor. A captive Huron, who had escaped from Onondaga arrived in Quebec at the same time as Father d'Ablon. He warned that the "Onondagas sole design was to attract to their country as many French and Hurons as possible and then to kill them in a general massacre" (J.R.43:129).

Many of the Hurons who were to accompany the French to the Onondagas retracted their word and:

> conjured us, by the love they bore us, not to cast ourselves into so manifest a danger. In addition to this cause of fear, the Agnieronnon [Mohawk] Iroquois, with whom we had recently concluded a treaty of peace, manifested a jealousy almost verging on fury, because we wished to dwell with those people; for it was greatly to the benefit of their trade, that the Onnontoeronnons [Onondagas] should always be compelled to pass through their country.
> . . All this added to the dangers and difficulties of the road, and to the excessive and frightful expenses that would have to be incurred to commence and maintain this undertaking, caused us extreme anxiety (J.R.43: 129, 131; Jennings 1984: 106-7).

On the other hand, the Governor warned:

> if the French rebuffed the invitation by refusing what they so urgently demanded, they might unite with the Mohawks

'to fall upon the French, to wage endless war against them, and, if possible, to exterminate them entirely' (J.R.43:131).

We were not at that time in a position to withstand the revolt of all those tribes, without running a greater danger than that of exposing a handful of French, whose resolution might exercise some restraint over those people in their own country (J.R.43:131).

French Decide to Send a Mission

The Fathers of our Society . . . said that they would surely, before their own death, baptize a number of dying persons equal to their own; in such case, they said, by giving their bodies for Souls, they would lose nothing by the exchange. They cited the example of the Apostles, who fully expected to lose their lives in the pagan countries whither they went to preach their Master, and yet they failed not to go there . . .

God who is the Master of the Great and of the lowly, of the French and the Iroquois, will touch the hearts of the Unbelievers to make them receive the Gospel (J.R.43:133).

On 17 May 1656, with the Onondagas as guides, the large expedition assembled at Quebec for the journey. The leader of the more than 40 French soldiers and workers was Zacharie Dupuis, formerly commandant of the fort at Quebec.

Accompanying Father Claude d'Ablon were five Jesuits: Father Rene Menard, Father Jacques Fremin, Brother Ambroise Broar, and Brother Joseph Boursier, as well as, Father Francois le Mercier, superior of the missions. In addition to Hurons, there were also Senecas, who were in Quebec after contracting an alliance for their people (J.R.43: 133,135; Jennings 1984:107).

As the two shallops and several canoes set off, a large multitude stood on the shore waving with compassion and hope. By the 20th, the expedition reached Three Rivers, and, on the 31st arrived at Montreal. A week later, on 8 June, they embarked in 20 canoes; the shallops could not be used in the rapids and falls that were ahead. In the lead canoe flew a fine white taffeta flag with J E S U S in large letters (J.R.43:139).

It was probably Father d'Ablon who continued to keep the daily journal. In any case, the writer noted that:

> upon entering Lake Saint Louys, one of our canoes was broken, an accident which happened several times during our voyage. We landed and our ship carpenters found everywhere material enough to build a vessel in less than a day. The architects of this country build their homes, palaces, and ships much more rapidly than those of Europe; and if one be not lodged there so sumptuously, still one often dwells there in greater comfort and gladness.
>
> We killed a number of elk and of the deer which our French call "wild cows." On 13 June and the three following days, we found ourselves in currents of water so rapid and strong that we were at times compelled to get into the water, in order to drag behind us, or carry on our shoulders, our boats and all our baggage. We were wet through and through; for, while one-half of our bodies was in the water, the sky saturated the other with a heavy rain (J.R.139,141).
>
> On 17 June we found ourselves at one end of a lake which some confound with Lake Saint Louys. We gave it the name of Saint Francois, to distinguish it from the one that precedes it. It is fully ten leagues long and three or four leagues wide in some places, and contains many beautiful islands at its mouths. The great river Saint Lawrence, widening and spreading its waters at various points, forms those beautiful Lakes, and then, narrowing its course, it once more assumes the name of River (J.R.43:139,141).

On the 20th, they passed the grand Sault. "Five fawns were killed by our hunters and a hundred catfish taken by our fishermen" (J.R.43:141).

However, for some days provisions ran low. As they approached Otiatannehengue [Salmon River], they expected to find large quantities of fish. However, there were none; the season was over by 3 July, so they sent ahead to Onondaga for provisions to be brought to them (J.R.43:145).

The only food available was a small wild fruit called Atoka (cranberry). Although the Indians are accustomed to remain for two or three days without food, all but five of the forty who started out left for their villages. The next two days, they caught some fish, but they were so few that they could give each of the sixty men only a rather small pike as a meal (J.R.43:145,147).

On the seventh, about ten o'clock at night, we reached the mouth of the river [Oswego], which forms Lake Gannentaa on the shores of which we intended to form our residence. When we awoke on the following day, we encountered currents of water so rapid that we had to exert all our strength and paddle vigorously in order to ascend. [The river rises 118 feet in the next fifteen miles. Seven locks enable boats to bypass the falls now.]

I must admit the faces of most of us, already wan and emaciated, appeared dejected to an extraordinary degree. At night, all our company lay down, having taken nothing but a drop of brandy; and in the morning, we had to start out and contend all day long against breakers, which made us recede almost as far as we advanced. In fact, we made only a league that day; for some of our people fell ill, and the others lost courage (J.R.43:147,149).

In this state of complete dejection we observed a canoe loaded with provisions coming toward us, which seemed to be propelled by wings instead of paddles. The sight cured nearly all our sick . . . we landed; and he who was the master of the convoy, after a short greeting, presented us, on behalf of the elders and Father Chaumonot with some sacks of Indian corn and some large salmon that had just been cooked. This small canoe was followed by two larger ones as well-filled as the first. We give thanks to God for granting us a succor so greatly needed. On every side kettles are

hanging over the fire, and there is naught but rejoicing
(J.R.43:149).

On 10 July at the place where they intended to spend the night, one of the leading Chiefs was waiting to welcome them on behalf of the Onondagas and the other tribes as well.

Arrival at Onondaga Lake

On 11 July 1656, at about 3 P.M., they reached the entrance to Lake Gannentaha (Onondaga) on the shores of which they intended to establish their residence (J.R.43:151). Father d'Ablon describes the special ceremonies:

> When we had advanced to a distance of a quarter of a league from the spot, we ourselves landed five small pieces of cannon, the light thunder of which we made resound along the waters of the lake; this was followed by the discharge of all the arquebuses in the hands of our people.
>
> Such was the first salute that we sent over the water, through the air, and through the woods, to the Elders of the country who were awaiting us with a great multitude of people. The noise rolled over the water, burst in the air and was most agreeably reechoed by the forests.
>
> After this we advanced in fine order, our canoes or small boats proceeding four by four along this little lake. On landing, our French fired a second discharge or salvo, so skillfully that they delighted all.
>
> The elders had caused two scaffolds to be erected from which to pay us their compliments aloud and to deliver to us their harangues. These were interrupted by a downpour of rain, which compelled us all to seek shelter. The words changed into caresses and manifestations of joy on both sides (J.R.43:157,159).

French Visit Onondaga Village

A few days later on 17 July the Jesuit writer described the special protocol of the visit of Father le Mercier and fifteen soldiers to the main village of the Onondagas. Located about five leagues away, it is thought to have been about two miles southeast of Manlius.

The people, who had been notified of the coming of the French, came forth in crowds to meet us. At a quarter of a league from the Village, some elders begged us to halt and take breath, in order to listen to a polite harangue, full of compliments, delivered to us by a Captain, one of the leading men of the country.

He then walked before us, and led us through a great crowd formed in ranks on both sides. We marched behind him quietly and in fine order, followed by another Captain, who came after us to prevent the great crowd from pressing too closely on us.

At the entrance to the Village, our soldiers fired a fine salvo, which delighted all the spectators. We were conducted to the cabin of one of the principal and most renowned Captains of the country, where everything was prepared for our reception in their fashion.

Fruit was brought to us from all sides; there was nothing but feasting; and for ten days all the game and fish of the village were used in regaling the French. All the families vied with one another as to which one should have us (J. R.43:161,163).

Envoys from other Iroquois nations arrived to pay their respects, and to hold a council to settle a quarrel between the Mohawks and the Senecas, as well as put something in the war kettle -- that is, to consult together about the means of attacking and defeating their enemies, and of contributing toward the general expenses. Father le Mercier was able to settle the quarrel amicably. All agreed "we should establish ourselves and reside in their country." (J.R.43:169).

We built a chapel at Onontague, to which some of our fathers were attached . . . We hardly ever ceased from morning to night to preach, to catechize, to baptize, to teach the prayers, and to answer the questions put to us on all sides. (J.R.43:181).

91

After the French returned to Sainte Marie on 27 July, the chief men of the Onondagas returned the visit of the French. They brought presents and warned the French not to place any confidence in the Mohawks.

They advised "fortifying ourselves well, and make our house large enough to receive and shelter them from their enemies in case of necessity" (J.R.43: 181).

Lack of concern about the environment over the years caused severe pollution of Onondaga Lake. Father d'Ablon's journal offers a vivid description of the lake and the surrounding territory as it was in the seventeenth century.

In size the Lake is about two leagues in length and half a league in width. We have observed three remarkable facts in connection with it.

The first is that, South of it, there are springs of salt water, although the lake itself is very far from the sea,- just as in Lorraine [France], where there are similar springs. But I do not think that salt can be obtained there with as much facility as here; for it is found ready-made on the soil and in the vicinity of those springs, and when the water is boiled, it is easily turned into salt.

The second is that, in the spring, so great numbers of passenger pigeons collect around these salt-springs, that sometimes as many as seven hundred are caught in the course of one morning.

The third remarkable fact is, that at the same place there are found certain snakes which are seen nowhere else. [These are still present today in nearby Cicero swamp]. We call them rattlesnakes, because, as they crawl along, they make a noise like that of a rattle,- or, rather of a cicada. At the end of their tails they have round scales, so joined with another, that, by opening and closing them, they make that noise, which is heard at a distance of twenty paces. These rattles or scales also make a noise when they are shaken after the death of the snake; but it is not so loud as that which the snake makes when alive.

The Natives say its scales are an excellent remedy for toothache, and that its flesh, which they find as well-flavored as that of the eel, cures fever. They cut off the tail and the head, which is quite flat and almost square, and eat the remainder. The body is about three feet long, thicker than a man's wrist, and all speckled on the back with black and yellow spots,- except on the tail, which is almost entirely black. It has four teeth, two above and two below, as long as our small needles, but much sharper. It bites like a dog, and injects its poison into the wound through a small black sting, which it draws out of a bag containing the poison.

When a person is bitten, he at once swells up, and, unless he receive prompt assistance, he dies in a short time, entirely covered with red pustules. When these snakes see a man, they hiss and shake their tails, sounding their rattles, either to frighten the enemy, or to excite themselves for the fight. . . . I know not whether these snakes are attracted by the salt; but I do know that the spot whereon we have erected our dwelling, and which is surrounded by fine springs of fresh water, is not infested by them, although it is on the shore of the same Lake (J.R. 43:151,153,155).

On Monday the seventeenth, we set to work in good earnest, to build lodgings for ourselves, and a good Redout for the soldiers, which we erected on an eminence commanding the Lake and all the surrounding places. There is an abundance of freshwater springs; and, in a word, the spot seems as beautiful as it is convenient and advantageous (J.R.43:161).

We landed on the edge of a forest which we had to cut away by dint of many heavy blows of our axes, in order to make room for the settlement that we wished to establish. But these great forests were guarded during the Summer, by little winged Dragons, - I mean, by innumerable legions of mosquitoes and Gnats, all very thirsty for a blood that they had never tasted; we were compelled to give way to them during the night, and to sleep on the rocks, on the shore of a lake, exposed to the air, to the wind, and frequently to the rain.

These labors - during the performance of which our only sustenance consisted of a little meal of Indian corn, boiled in clear water prostrated nearly all of us. More than forty-eight of our people fell sick [malaria from the mosquitoes?]. We had to lodge under rocks, where we had so little room, that we lay almost in a heap, one upon another. While one was burning in the heat of fever, another shivered with cold, and to console us, we were often told, by people from various places that men were coming to kill us, and that we would soon be delivered from all our ills (J.R.43:87).

At the height of their misery and privations fish and game became plentiful before the usual season and the sick were relieved and strengthened. The Onondagas brought them beans and squashes, which they considered firmer and better than those of France. They also brought fresh ears of their corn . . . showing every possible kindness during the illness of the French. Thus, they all recovered (J.R.43:183).

Onondaga Lake Area As It Was
Father d'Ablon vividly described the scene before him:

Our residence is situated between the 42nd and 43rd degrees, on the shores of the little Lake Gannentaa . . . one of the most commodious and most agreeable dwelling-places in the world, without excepting even the levee of the River Loire . . .

It has advantages that are wanting in the rest of Canada; for besides grapes, plums, and many other fruits, - which it has in common with the fine Provinces of Europe, it has a number of others, which excel ours in beauty, fragrance, and taste. The forests consist almost entirely of chestnut and walnut trees.

There are two kinds of nuts; one kind [shell- bark hickory, C. alba, or the "pig-nut," C. glabra] is as sweet

94

and agreeable to the taste as the other [swamp hickory, C. Amara] is bitter; but, with all their bitterness, an excellent oil is extracted from them by passing them through the ashes, through the mill, through fire, and through water, in the same way as the Indians extract oil from sunflowers.

Stoneless cherries [cranberries] are found there. Fruits grow there which are of the color and size of an apricot [May-apple - Podophyllum peltatum], whose blossom is like that of the white lily, and which smell and taste like the citron.

There are apples as large as a goose's egg [papaw - Asimina triloba]; the seed had been brought from the country of the Cats and looks like beans; the fruit is delicate and has a very sweet smell; the trunk is of the height and thickness of our dwarf trees; it thrives in swampy spots and in good soil.

But the most common and most wonderful plant in those countries is that which we call the universal plant [Laurus Sassafras], because its leaves, when pounded, heal in a short time wounds of all kind. These leaves, which are as broad as one's hand, have the shape of a lily as depicted in heraldry; and its roots have the smell of the laurel.

The most vivid scarlet, the brightest green, the most natural yellow and orange of Europe pale before the various colors that the Iroquois procure from roots.

I say nothing of trees [elm] as tall as oaks, whose leaves are as large and as open as those of cabbages; or of many other plants, peculiar to this country, because as yet we are ignorant of their properties.

The springs, which are as numerous as they are wonderful, are nearly all mineral. Our little lake, which is only six or seven leagues in circumference, is almost entirely surrounded by salt springs. The water is used for salting and seasoning meat, and for making very good salt. It often forms of itself in fine crystals with which nature takes pleasure in surrounding these springs.

95

The salt that forms at a spring about two days' journey from our residence toward Oiogoen [the Cayugas], is much stronger than that from the springs of Gannentaa; for when the water - which looks as white as milk, and the smell of which is perceptible from a great distance - is boiled, it leaves a kind of salt almost as corrosive as caustic. The rocks about that spring are covered with a foam as thick as cream.

The spring in the direction of the Sonnontouan [Senecas] is no less wonderful; for its water - being of the same nature as the surrounding soil, which has only to be washed in order to obtain perfectly pure sulphur - ignites when shaken violently, and yields sulphur when boiled.

As one approaches nearer the country of the Cats, one finds heavy and thick water, which ignites like brandy, and boils up in bubbles of flame when fire is applied to it. It is, more- over, so oily that all our Indians use it to anoint and grease their heads and their bodies.

One must not be astonished at the fertility of this country, for it is everywhere watered by Lakes, Rivers and Springs, which are found even on the highest mountains. But if these waters make the earth fertile, they themselves are none the less fruitful in what pertains to them.

The fish most commonly found in them are eels and salmon, which are caught there from the spring to the end of autumn. The Iroquois construct their dams and sluices so well that they catch at the same time the eels, that descend, and the salmon, that always ascend. In the Lakes, they catch fish in a different manner; they spear them with a trident by the light of a bituminous fire, which they maintain in the bows of their canoes (J.R.43:257,259, 261,324,325).

The Jesuit writer noted that:

the Onondagas possess virtues which might cause shame to most Christians. No hospitals are needed among

96

them, because there are neither mendicants nor paupers, as long as there are any rich people among them. Their kindness, humanity, and courtesy not only make them liberal with what they have, but cause them to possess hardly anything except in common.

A whole village must be without corn, before any individual can be obliged to endure privation. They divide the produce of their fisheries equally with all who come; and the only reproach they address to us is our hesitation to send to them oftener for our supply of provisions (J.R.43:271,273).

Living close to the Onondagas, the French lost their fear of attack. They found them kind and considerate. Father wrote that "not one of us was ill last winter, without their manifesting that they shared his trouble by giving him liberally of their game, just as they afterward showed by their presents the joy which they felt at his recovery" (J.R.43:275,277).

After Father le Mercier, called Achiendase by the Iroquois, contracted an alliance with Sagochiendagesite, a chief of the Onondagas, they treated the French as faithful friends (J.R.43:277).

Iroquois Condolence Ceremony

When two of the French died, the chief men among them conducted their traditional ceremony uttering mournful cries of consolation. He who carried the presents of condolence - eight collars of porcelain beads - addressed himself to the Father Superior, saying:

The elders of our country have the custom of wiping away one another's tears when they are afflicted by any misfortune. We come, Achiendase, to perform that friendly duty toward thee. We weep with thee, because misfortune cannot touch thee without piercing us by the same blow; and we cannot, without extreme regret, see thee suffer so in our country, after having left thine own, where thou wert perfectly comfortable. Sickness casts

97

thy nephews into the depths of a land whose extent thou knowest not yet.

Ah, how the cruel Demon seizes the opportunity to afflict those whom he hates! To do that evil deed, he chooses the very moment when thou hast the greatest need of thy nephews to build thy cabins, to fortify thyself, and to till thy fields.

After harassing them in vain throughout the Summer, and finding himself too weak to attack thee, he has leagued himself with the Demons of fever and death, in order to add our loss to yours, and to work havoc among us still more than among you. But take courage, our brother; we wipe away the tears from thine eyes, that thou mayst see that not all thy nephews are dead.

We open thine eyes with this present, that thou mayst consider those who are left to thee, and by thy pleasant looks restore life and joy to them at the same time.

As to our two nephews who are dead, they must not go naked into the other world; here are fine graveclothes wherewith to cover them. Here is something also wherewith to place them in their graves, to prevent the sight of them from renewing thy grief, and to remove all sorts of lugubrious objects away from thy eyes. This present is to level the earth in which I have placed them; and this other one, to erect a palisade around their grave, in order that the flesh-eating animals and birds may not disturb their rest.

Finally, this last present is to calm thy mind and restore it to its seat that our peace may continue as firm as before, and that no Demon may impair it (J.R.43:277,279,281).

The next year Father Ragueneau wrote to Rev. Jacques Renault 21 August 1658, that nearly 500 children and a number of adults died, usually after baptism (J.R.44:155; Jennings,109). Their losses far outnumbered the few deaths of the French. Yet, these Iroquois generously extended their sympathy, according to their time-honored custom, even to those who may have brought the diseases to them.

Rev. Paul Ragueneau S. J.

Evidently an epidemic came to the Onondagas at the same time as the mission. The population of the Onondagas at this time is unknown. One source in 1660 estimated 300 warriors and a total population of five times that (Jennings,35; Michelson, Table 1, p.4; 3,000 according to Radisson,95).

The Native Americans had no immunity to diseases such as smallpox, measles, diphtheria, typhoid, etc. These caused a massive decline in their numbers. One study estimated that for one who lived early in the twentieth century about seventy-two existed four centuries earlier in North America (Dobyns, 343).

Before the age of modern medicine, the cause and cure of illnesses was attributed to many sources. Some believed sickness came from actions of demons that entered the body and must be expelled. Therapy was by exorcism or incantation. Another source was punishment for an evil deed or magic poison from an evil creature. Bloodletting was a French cure. Medicines included purgatives, emetics and herbal solutions. Many of these are the basis of medicines used today.

It was not until 1796 that Edward Jenner first demonstrated that vaccination with cowpox provides immunity to smallpox. During the last half of the 19th century the investigations of Pasteur, Koch, Lister, etc., identified specific bacteria as the cause of anthrax, typhoid, diphtheria, tuberculosis, etc.

99

7

Radisson Joins the Resupply Expedition

The next summer it was necessary to send a second expedition to resupply Sainte Marie. Some of the Hurons, who had fled their homes in previous years, had been living near Montreal. Under pressure from the Iroquois, they had agreed to divide themselves; some staying with the French, some joining the Mohawks, and some going to live at Onondaga. Fulfilling the previous year's agreement, a number of Onondagas arrived in Montreal to escort the Hurons.

Joining the expedition also were two Jesuits, Fathers Paul Ragueneau and Francois du Peron, as well as several Frenchmen including Peter Esprit Radisson (J.R.44:187).

Earlier, Radisson had been captured by the Mohawks and lived in their village for several months, learning the language and the customs. Some time later he wrote an account of his travels. In the following excerpts he describes his experiences on this journey (Radisson 94-134).

Leaving Montreal on 26 July 1657, there were over 200 divided among 30 boats. Radisson estimates there were 80 Iroquois, some hundred Huron women and some 10 or 12 Huron men, 20 French with two Jesuits. However, thirty of the Iroquois left after the first day (Radisson, 97).

To pass the rapids it was necessary to carry (portage) the canoes and provisions over land. Radisson explains:

> we draw the boats loaden after us, and when there is not water enough, everyone his bundle by land. . . . We entered another lake somewhat bigger, it's called S'francis . . . . I assure you it is a delightfull and beautiful country. We wanted nothing to the view passing those skirts, killing staggs, and fowles. As for the fish, what a thing it is to see them in the bottom of the water and take it biting the hook or lancing it with lance or cramp iron (Radisson, 98).

Hunting Along the St. Lawrence

Radisson traveled in a canoe with an Iroquois:

> a young man taller and properer than myself . . . childish
> and young as I. As for meat, we wanted none, and we had
> store of large staggs along the water side. We killed some
> almost every day, more from sport than for need. We
> finding them sometimes in islands, made them go into the
> water and after we killed about a score, we clipped the
> ears of the rest and hung a bell to it, and then let them
> loose. What a sport to see the rest fly from those which
> had the bell! (Radisson,103, 104).

Radisson found a kind of billboard of news in the forest as
they were passing up the St. Lawrence:

> Going along the woodside we came where a great many
> trees were cut, as if it were intended for a fort. At the
> end of it there was a tree left standing, but the rind
> [bark] taken away from it. Upon it there was painted
> with a coal 6 men hanged, with their heads at their feet,
> cut off. They were so well drawn, that the one of them
> was father [priest] by the shortness of his hair, which let
> us know that the French that was before us were
> executed.
>   A little further on, another was painted of two boats,
> one of three men, another of two, whereof one was
> standing with a hatchet in his hands striking on the
> head. At another were represented seven boats pursuing
> three bears, a man drawn as if he were on land with his
> gun shooting a stag (Radisson, 108).

Later, he learned that the marks they had seen on the trees
were done by the Mohawks that came back from the wars in the
north. They met two boats of Hurons going to live with the
French. Of the Hurons, six were slain, one taken alive and the
other escaped (Radisson,113).

101

The next day they "make up our bundles in readiness to wander upon that sweet sea as is the saying of the Iroquois, who rekens by their day's journey" (Radisson,114).

Surviving a Storm on Lake Ontario
However, he next describes how they narrowly escaped drowning when a sudden storm overtakes them while crossing Lake Ontario:

Seeing the water so calme and faire, we ventured some 3 leagues to gaine a point of the firme land, that by that means we should shorten 7 or 8 leagues in our way. We went on along the lake in this manner with great delight, sometimes with paine and labour.

As we went along the water side, the weather very faire, it comes to my mind to put out a cover instead of a saile. My companion liked it very well . . . We seeing that our sayle made us goe faster than the other boat, not perceiving that the wind came from the land, which carried us far into the lake, our companions made a signe, having more experience than wee, and judged of the weather that was to come. We would not heare them, thinking to have an advantage.

Soone after the wind began to blow harder, made us soone strike sayle, and putt our armes to work. We feeled not the wind because it was in our backs, but turning aside, we finde that we have enough to doe. We must gett ourselves to a better element then that [where] we were.

Instantly comes a shower of raine with a storme of winde that was able to perish us by reason of the great quantity of watter that came into our boat. . . .Seeing we went backwards rather than forwards, we thought ourselves utterly lost.

That rogue that was with me said, "See thy God that thou sayest he is above. Will you make me believe now that he is good, as the black-coats [the father Jesuits] say? They doe lie, and you see the contrary; for first,

102

you see that the sun burns us often, the raine wetts us, the wind makes us have shipwrake, the thundering, the lightnings burns and kills, and all come from above, and you say that it's good to be there.

For my part I will not go there. Contrary they say that the reprobats and guilty goeth downe and burne. They are mistaken; all is good heare. Doe not you see the earth that nourishes all living creatures, the water, the fishes, and the yus, and that corn and all other seasonable fruits for our food, which things are not so contrary to us as that from above?" ...

He took his instruments and showed them to the heavens, saying, "I will not be above; here will [I] stay on earth, where all my friends are, and not with the French, that are to be burned above with torments" (Radisson,114,115).

Radisson did not answer, but reveals his thoughts in the following comments and describes how they escaped drowning:

How should one think to escape this torments and storms, but God who through his tender mercy ceas'd the tempest and gave us strength to row till we came to the side of the water? I may call it a mighty storm by reason of the littleness of the boat, which are all in watter to the breadth of five fingers or less.

I thought uppon it, and out of distress made a vertue to seek the means to save ourselves. We tyed a sack full of corn in the fore end of our boat, and threw it into the watter, which hung downe some foure fathoms, and wee putt our selves in the other end, so that the end that was towards the wind was higher than the other, and by that means escaped the waves that without doubt, if we have not used that means, we had sunk'd. The other boat landed to let the storm [pass] over. We found them in the even[ing] att their cottages, and [they] thought [it was] impossible for us to escape (Radisson,115,116).

Arrival at Sainte Marie

A few days later, when they were within 30 leagues of their destination, three people from the fort came to meet them and guide them the rest of the way. Radisson described their arrival at Sainte Marie on Lake Onondaga as follows:

> Having come to the landing place att the foot of the fort, we found there a most faire castle very neatly built, 2 great and 2 small ones. The bottom was built with great trees and well tyed in the top with twiggs of ashure, strengthened with two strong walles and 2 bastions, which made the fort impregnable ...
>
> There was also a fine fall of woods about it. The French corne [wheat] grew there exceedingly well, where was as much as covered half a league of land.
>
> The country smooth like a boord, a matter of some 3 or 4 leagues about. Several fields of all sides of Indian corn, several of french tournaps [turnips], full of chestnuts and oakes of acorns with thousand such like fruit in abundance. A great company of hoggs so fatt that they were not able to goe. A plenty of all sorts of fowles. The ringdoves [passenger pigeons] in such a number that in a net 15 or 1600 att once might be taken. So this was not a wild country to our imagination, but plentyfull in every thing (Radisson,118).

He counted forty Frenchmen, "as well domestiques as volontiers," at the fort, in addition to the Jesuit Fathers. However, all the arrivals immediately became ill with a fever, (malaria again?) just as the previous expedition had experienced. "Some continued a month, some more, and some less, which is the tribut that one must pay for the change of climate" (Radisson,118,119).

Shortly after the expedition left Montreal, three Frenchmen had been killed. French farms had been pillaged and cattle destroyed. Raiding Iroquois war parties were suspected. French farmers were demanding action (J.R.44:155, 193; Jennings 1984, 107).

At Montreal three Oneidas visited the Governor, Monsieur de Maisonneuve. They protested their innocence and deep regret at the outrage committed upon the French. They offered seven presents of porcelain collars in traditional Iroquois custom of concern for victims. The Governor received them but asked them to stay nearby (J.R.44:195).

At Quebec, the newly-appointed French Governor in command over all the French, Monsieur d'Ailleboust, suspected that Mohawks were the Iroquois warriors to blame. Having no experience in dealing with life on the frontier in New France, he overreacted.

Arrest of Iroquois

He ordered "the arrest, throughout the French settlements of all the Iroquois that should present themselves, from whatever quarter they might come." Several Mohawks were seized at Three Rivers and sent on to Quebec. This action by the Governor was to have far-reaching repercussions. (J.R.44:155, 193, 197).

The Governor held a council with the French and their Indian allies to announce a plan. As Father le Moyne was presently at the Mohawk villages, the Governor wished to inform him that some Mohawks had been detained, that three Frenchmen had been killed and that the relatives of the deceased wished to take vengeance on the Mohawks. He sent the message with two Mohawks that had been arrested.

The Governor stressed that no harm would be done to those he had detained. "We are resolved to hold them during the journey of those whom we send to complain of this outrage to the elders of the country and to learn whether it was not committed by their young men. Assurance is given that those who are held in custody will be well-treated" (J.R.44:197,199).

Additional messages were sent to Onondaga to inform them of the problem. However, these never arrived (J.R. 44: 201).

The Mohawk warriors, in particular, felt the imprisonment of their men by the French was unjust. In revenge, it was rumored they would attack the mission at Onondaga. One of the elders at Onondaga, who was ill and dying, asked for baptism by the

Fathers. He confided this rumor to them (J.R.44:187, 189,215; Radisson,123).

Plans to Abandon Sainte Marie

As a result, Radisson noted:

> we must resolve to be uppon our guard, being in the midle of our Ennemy. For this purpose we begin to make provisions for the future end. . . We seeing no other remedy but must be gon[e] and leave a delightful country. The onely thing that wee wanted most was that we had no boats to carry our bagage. It is sad to tend from such a place that is compassed with those great lakes that compose that Empire that can be named the greatest part of the knowne world. At last they contrived some deale boords to make ships with large bottoms, which was the cause of our destruction sooner than was expected.
>
> You have heard it said how the fathers inhabited the hurron country to instruct them in Christian doctrine. They preach the mighty power of the Almighty, who had drowned the world for to punish the wicked, saving onely Noah with his family in an arke (Radisson,124).

A young Indian named Jaluck saw the boards and thought the French were making another ark to escape their hands and:

> by our inventions cause all the rest to be drowned in a second deluge . . . All frightened, [he] runns to his village, makes them all afraid. Each talkes of it. The elders gathered together to consult what was to be done. In their councell [it] was concluded that our fort should be visited, that our fathers should be examined, and according to their answers deliberation should be taken to preserve both their life and countrey (Radisson,124-125).

A batteaux then upon the dock was almost finished. To avoid causing suspicions, the French made a double floor in the hall where the ship was abuilding, making a ceiling, as it were, and raising the boat up above into the attic, so that the Indians could not see it (Radisson,125).

From then on they hid everything that would raise questions by any of their Indian visitors. Both boats were finally finished in secret. These boats drew very little water and carried a heavy load - fourteen or fifteen men and fifteen or sixteen hundred livres [pounds] in weight (J.R. 44:175,177).

> So done, finding nothing that was reported, all began to be quiet and out of feare. . . . We kept them secretly and covered them with 12 boats of rind [bark] which we kept for fishing and hunting. The Indians knewed of these small things but [the French thought] suspected nothing, believing the French would never . . . venture such a voyage for the difficultie of the way and violence of the swiftnesse of the rivers and length of the way. We stayed for opportunity in some quietness, devising to contrive our game as soone as the spring should begin (Radisson, 125,126).

Later, Father Ragueneau wrote to the Father Procuror for the Missions of the Society of Jesus in New France:

> The difficulty was to embark unperceived by the Iroquois, who constantly beset us. The conveyance of the boats, canoes, and all the equipment, could not be accomplished without much noise; and yet, without secrecy, there was nothing to hope for but a general massacre of our whole company, at the moment when it should be perceived that we had the least thought of taking our departure (J.R.44:177).

Radisson continued:

> The season drawing nigh we must think of some strategeme to escape their hands and the rest of ours [French] that weare [were] among them; which was a

107

difficulty, because they would have some of us by them always for the better assurance. . . .

We let them understand that the time drew neere that the french uses to trait [treat] their friends in feasting and meriment, and all should be welcome, having no greater friends than they were. . . . The considerablest persons are invited, the father and two French. There they weare made much of 2 days with great joy, with sounds of trompetts, drumms and flageoletts[similar to a flute], with songs in French as [well as] Indian.

So done, they are sent away, the father with them. He was not a mile off but fains to gett a falle and sighed that his arme was broken (Radisson,126,127).

They brought the father back and made gifts that he may be cured. A plaster was set to his arm and he was put to bed. All the Indians came to see him; he encouraged them that he should soon recover and see them. All retired to their village and the French sought the means to embark (Radisson,126-127).

The French agreed to a plan for another feast after the lake was opened from the ice and they had everything ready for their purpose. It would be to celebrate the safe recovery of the "injured" father's health (J.R.44:177; Radisson,127).

Importance of Dreams

According to the French observations, dreams were very important to many of the Iroquois. They considered them a message from the spirit world. "It would be cruelty, nay, murder, not to give a man the subject of his dream if at all possible; for such a refusal might cause his death" (J.R.42:165).

One of the elders at Onondaga had adopted one of the young Frenchmen. He was persuaded to go to his Indian "father" and say he had just dreamed of one of those feasts where all served up must be eaten. He begged him to give one of that kind to the whole village; and he told him that he had the impression on his mind, that if anything was left, he would die.

The elder replied that he would be very sorry to see him die; he should himself order the feast, but that he [elder] would take care of the invitations and make sure that nothing would be left. On this promise the young man fixed the 19th of March for his feast, being the day set for departure (Charlevoix III: 16,17).

Some of the French did not believe that they were in any danger. Many of the Indians were so kind to them bringing food, attending prayers of the Jesuit fathers, inviting many of them to their cabins. But even some of their friends whispered of those who blamed the ruin of the Hurons on the Jesuits. They blamed them for the spread of disease which killed so many (Radisson,122,123).

Dancing and Feasting at Sainte Marie

At last, after sundown on 19 March all was ready. The trumpets blew to summon 100 elders and as many women. No one had been permitted to visit the mission during the day. Radisson explained that:

> it was not our custom to show the splendour of our banquetts before they should be presented att table. . . Everyone made his bundle of provisions and merchandise and household stuff, gunns, & c., some hid in the ground and the rest scattered because we could not save them.
>
> The evening being come, the Indians are brought to the place destinated, not far from our fort.
>
> We made excellent bisquetts of the last year's corn, and forgot not the hoggs that were a fatning . . . There is nothing but outcryes, clapping of hands, and capering, that they may have better stomach to their meat. There comes a dozen of great kettles full of beaten Indian corne dressed with mince meat. The wisest begins his speech, giving heaven thanks to have brought such generous French to honnour them so.
>
> . . . Heare comes 2 great kettles full of bustards [Canada Geese], broyled and salted before the winter, with as many kettles full of ducks. As many turtles were taken in

109

the season by the net. . . and other sort comes, as divers of fish, eels, salmon, and carps. . .

The best is that we are sure none will forske his place, nor man nor woman. A number of french entertaines them, keeping them from sleepe in dancing and singing, for that is the custome.

Their lutrill, an instrumental musick, is much heere in use. Yet nothing is done as yett, for there comes the thickened flower, the oyl of bears, venison. To this the knife is not enough, the spunes also are used (Radisson,128-129).

He who presided at the ceremony played his part with such skill and success that each one was bent on contributing to the public joy. They vied with one another in uttering piercing yells, now of war, now of glee; while out of complaisance, the Onondagas sang and danced in the French manner [minuet ?], and the French in that of the Onondagas.

To encourage them more and more in this fine game, presents were distributed to those who best played their parts, and who made the most noise for drowning that made outside by two-score of our men in transporting our outfit (J.R.44: 177).

Radisson continued:

We bid them cheare up and tould them it was an usual custome with the french to make much of themselves and of their friends. . . Cheer up like brave men. If your sleepe overcomes you, you must awake; come, sound [the] drumme, it is not now to beat the Gien [play the guitar]; come, make a noise. . . .

In the end nothing [is] spared that can be invented to the greater confusion. There is strife between the french who will make the greatest noise. But there is an end to all things; the houre is come, for all is embarked. The Indians can hold out no longer; they must sleep. They cry out "Skenon," enough, we can bear no more. . . They are told that the french are weary and will sleepe also awhile. They say, "Be it so." We come away; all is quiet. Nobody makes a noise after such a hurly-burly. The fort is shutt up, as if we had been in it. We leave a hogg at the door for sentry, with a rope tyed to his foot"(Radisson,129, 130; Charlevoix,III:17).

French Leave Sainte Marie

Some of the French [soldiers?] proposed killing the 100 Onondaga men, the 100 women and children nearby and then go to their village to deal with 5 or 600 women and maybe 1,000 children, while the young men were away hunting. It would be a revenge because of their disloyalty, breaking the peace and watching the opportunity to do the same.

The fathers' answer was this, "that they were sent to instruct the people in the faith of Jesus Christ and not to destroy; that the cross must be their sword" (Radisson,130).

Radisson wrote:

So to be obedient to our superiors without noise of trompet or drum, but zeal with griefe, we left that place. We are all embarked, and now must looke for the mouth of the river; and weare put to it, for it frized every night and the ice of good thicknesse, and consequently danger- ous to venture our boats against it.

We must all the way break the ice with great staves to make a passage. This gave us paines enough. Att the breake of day we were in sight att the mouth of the river, where we weare free from ice.

If those had but the least suspicion or had looked out, they had seen us. We soon by all diligence putt ourselves out of that apprehension, and came at the first rising of the river, where freed from ice ten leagues from the fort, where we kept a good watch (Radisson,131).

After a difficult journey through the snow, the ice, the rapids, the falls, they came to Montreal on 3 April 1658 (Radisson,131-133; J.R.44:17).

111

One of the tales the French heard later about the aftermath and the search for them was as follows:

> At length, night giving place to day, darkness to light, and sleep to awakening, these Indians issued from their cabins, walked about our house, which was securely locked, and wondered at the Frenchmen's utter silence. They saw no one come forth to go to work, they heard no voice. At first they thought that all were at prayers or in council; but, as the day advanced and the prayers did not reach an end, they knocked at the door, and the dogs, purposely left behind by our Frenchmen, gave answering yelps,. The crowing of the cock which they had heard in the morning, together with the noise of these dogs made them think that the masters of these animals were not far away, and they recovered their lost patience; but at length, the sun beginning to decline and no one answering either the voices of the men or the cries of the animals, they climbed into the house to see in what state our people were amid this fearful silence.
>
> Here their wonder was changed to alarm and perturbation. They opened the door; the chiefs entered, and went all over the house, ascending to the loft and going down into the cellar; but not a Frenchman appeared, alive or dead (J.R. 44:311,313,315).

The clan mothers had had no share in the plot. They had for a whole week mourned with their children over the departure of the missionaries (Charlevoix III:36).

Eventually some of their warriors and ambassadors were sent to the French territory to gain tidings of their guests and to recover their countrymen who had been put in irons (J. R.44:315).

The next April three Oneida ambassadors arrived in Quebec to admit responsibility for killing the three Frenchmen, to obtain release of the prisoners, and to deliberate on establishing a lasting peace. (Thus the Mohawks anger over the imprisonment of their men is understandable.)

The Oneidas carried a message from the Onondagas:

> The Onondagas remind thee that you had clasped each other by the arm; that you had bound yourselves with iron bonds. It is thou, frenchman, who hast broken the bond by departing from my country without my knowledge and by abandoning thy dwelling.
>
> The Onondagas take thee once more by the arm and renew friendship with thee more strongly than ever.
>
> The Onondagas say to thee "I give thee back thy house of Gannentaa; thy lodgings are still standing. An elder resides there to preserve them. Put thy canoe into the water, and go to take possession of what belongs to thee" (J.R. 45:85).

In July, 1661 Father le Moyne returned to the village of the Onondagas to escort some of their people whom the French had held captive, and, in exchange, free some French also being held hostage. He was welcomed and they had already built a chapel for him (J.R.46:156).

In August of 1669 Rev. Jacques Fremin, upon returning to the scene of his earlier endeavors refers to the abandoned "Mission" at Onondaga being "in the same condition . . ." as when he left it in 1658 (J.R.54:111).

113

Bibliography

Berkhofer, Robert F. Jr.
1978   *The White Man's Indian.* Alfred A. Knopf. N. Y.
 Bishop, Morris.
1948   *Champlain, The Life of Fortitude.* Alfred A. Knopf. New York.
Bradley, James.
1987   *Evolution of the Onondaga Iroquois.* Syracuse University
        Press, Syracuse, New York.
Burrage, Henry S. ed.
1906   *Early English and French Voyages 1534-1608.* Original
        Narratives of Early American History. Charles Scribner's
        Sons, New York.
Cartier, Jacques.
1890   *Jacques Cartier and his Four Voyages to Canada.* ed. Hiram
        B. Stephens. Drysdale & Co. Montreal.
1953   "Brief Recit" in *Jacques Cartier et "La Grosse Maladie."*
        Translated by Jean L. Launay. Montreal: XIXe Congres
        International de Physiologie, Montreal.
Champlain, Samuel de.
1907   *Voyages of Samuel de Champlain 1604-1618.* ed. W. L.
        Grant. Charles Scribner's Sons. 1907
1922-36 *Works of Samuel de Champlain* ed. H. P. Biggar. Champlain
        Society reprint University of Toronto Press
Charlevoix, Pierre-Francois-Xavier de, S. J.
1866-187 *History and General Description of New France.* Tr. John
         Gilmary Shea. 6 vols. New York. Francis P. Harper, 1900.
Connors, Dennis J., Gordon C. DeAngelo, Peter P. Pratt .
1980   *The Search for the Jesuit Mission of Ste. Marie de
        Gannentaha.* County of Onondaga, Office of Museums and
        Historical Sites.
Dobyns, Henry F.
1983   *Their Number Became Thinned.* University of Tennessee
        Press, Knoxville, Tenn.
Fenton, William N. ed.
1968   *Parker on the Iroquois.* Syracuse University Press, Syracuse,
        New York.

Jameson, John Franklin, ed.

1909   *Narratives of New Netherland 1609-1664.* Charles Scribner's
        Sons, New York.

Jennings, Francis.

1984   *The Ambiguous Iroquois Empire.* W. W. Norton. New York.

Jennings, Francis, et al.

1985   *History and Culture of Iroquois Diplomacy.* Syracuse
        University Press, Syracuse, New York.

Michelson , Gunther.

1977   "Iroquois Population Statistics" in *Man in the Northeast* 14.

Morgan, Lewis Henry

1851   *League of the Iroquois.* Reprint 1962. Corinth Books. New
        York.

1881   *Houses and House-life of the American Aborigines.* Reprint
        1965. University of Chicago Press, Chicago and London.

O'Callaghan, Edmund B., ed.

1949   *The Documentary History of the State of New York.* Weed,
        Parsons,& Co. Albany, New York.

Radisson, Peter Esprit

1885   *Voyages of Peter Esprit Radisson.* ed. Gideon D. Scull.
        Prince Society. Reprint. 1967 Burt Franklin, New York.

Ray, Arthur J. and Donald Freeman.

1978   *Give Us Good Measure.* University of Toronto Press,
        Toronto.

Richter, Daniel K.

1992   *The Ordeal of the Longhouse,* published for the Institute of
        Early American History and Culture, Williamsburg, Virginia
        by University of North Carolina Press, Chapel Hill, North
        Carolina.

Sturtevant, William C. ed.

1978   *Handbook of North American Indians* vol. 15 Smithsonian
        Institution, Washington, D. C.

Thwaites, Reuben Gold, ed.

1896-1901 *The Jesuit Relations and Allied Documents: Travels and
        Explorations of the Jesuit Missionaries in New France 1610-
        1791.* 73 vols. Burrows Bros. Co., Cleveland, Ohio.

Trelease, Allen W.

1960   *Indian Affairs in Colonial New York: The Seventeenth
        Century,* Cornell University Press. Ithaca, N.Y.

Trigger, Bruce G.
1978   "Early Iroquoian Contacts with Europeans" in *Handbook of North American Indians, the Northeast,* vol. 15 B. G. Trigger,
        ed., pp. 44-56. Washington D.C.:The Smithsonian Institution.
Woodbury, Hanni, ed.
1992   *Concerning the League,* Memoir 9, Algonquin and Iroquoian Linguistics, 1992.

Index